James Martin's
EASY BRITISH FOOD

James Martin's

EASY BRITISH FOOD

MITCHELL BEAZLEY

Dedication To my late, great Granny Smith

Easy British Food
by James Martin

First published in Great Britain in 2005
by Mitchell Beazley, an imprint of Octopus
Publishing Group Ltd, 2–4 Heron Quays,
London E14 4JP

Reprinted 2006

A CIP catalogue record for this book is available
from the British Library.

ISBN-13: 978 1 84000 977 4
ISBN-10: 1 84000 977 2

Commissioning Editor: Rebecca Spry
Executive Art Editor: Yasia Williams-Leedham
Project Manager: Vanessa Kendell
Design: Grade Design Consultants
Editor: Susan Fleming
Proofreader: Siobhán O'Connor
Production: Seyhan Essen
Home economist: Linda Tubby
Prop stylist: Sue Rowlands
Photographs: Jean Cazals
Index: John Noble

Typeset in New Baskerville and News Gothic

Printed and bound by Toppan Printing Company
in China

CONTENTS

Introduction

I'VE COOKED IN ALL SORTS OF PLACES, from student kitchens to grand hotels, and with all sorts of people, from mates to top chefs. And if there's one thing I've learned, it's that everyone loves a short cut. Let's face it, when the sun's out, the kids want you to play with them or the football's on the telly, why not cheat a bit to cut down on time spent in the kitchen?

Over the years I've developed lots of great ideas for 'instant' versions of our national favourites. It might just be a case of using shop-bought pastry instead of making your own, or making the most of time-saving ingredients such as easy-blend yeast or Bisto gravy powder. Some people turn their noses up at the idea of cheating like this – so let them spend hours in the kitchen while you have the fun, because easy food can be brilliant food, too!

The other piece of advice I always give people is to keep an eye on what's in season. After all, why mess about with making complicated dishes when you can cook really tasty fresh ingredients simply? Nothing beats a simple roast, poached seasonal fish or a fruit fool made with seasonal fruit, cream and sugar.

This book brings together the simplest dishes and tricks I've learned in restaurant kitchens – in particular as a pastry chef, when I picked up lots of ideas for making easy but impressive cakes, tarts and biscuits – and some of the best recipes passed on to me by my mum and gran. Some people won't consider lots of the recipes I've included to be 'British', but we've been eating stuff like curries and pizzas for as long as I can remember, so I reckon we've officially adopted them now. Anyway, this is a book about good living and good eating. And you can't ask for anything better than that.

James x

BREAKFASTS

Fortune's fish curers in Whitby

Eggs Benedict with Smoked Haddock

I REMEMBER COOKING THIS AT COLLEGE and wondering why we spent a whole day learning how to poach an egg. Now I know, as I have asked everybody I have interviewed since then to do it, and probably 50 per cent of them make a mess of it. Why? Because most of them are too busy thinking about the next fancy garnish to go on their plate, and not about what is really important. Good cooking is all about getting the basics right, and doing them well, before progressing. Delia, you are correct, and I thank you.

SERVES 4

300ml (10fl oz) milk
3 bay leaves
2 slices onion
6 black peppercorns
4 x 100g (3½oz) pieces thick
  undyed smoked haddock fillet
1 tbsp white wine vinegar
4 free-range eggs

TO SERVE AND GARNISH
2 English muffins
1 quantity hollandaise sauce
  (see page 138)
a few coarsely crushed black
  peppercorns
a few chopped chives

1 Make the hollandaise sauce and keep it warm, off the heat, over a pan of warm water.

2 Bring the milk and 300ml (10fl oz) of water to the boil in a shallow pan. Add the bay leaves, onion, peppercorns and smoked haddock pieces, bring back to a simmer and poach for 4 minutes. Lift the haddock out on to a plate, peel off the skin, discard any bones and keep warm.

3 Bring about 5cm (2in) water to the boil in a medium-sized pan, add the vinegar and reduce it to a gentle simmer. Break the eggs into the pan one at a time, and poach for 3 minutes.

4 Meanwhile, slice the muffins in half and toast them until lightly browned. Lift the poached eggs out of the water with a slotted spoon and drain briefly on kitchen paper.

5 To serve, place the muffin halves on to four warmed plates and top with the haddock and poached eggs. Spoon over the hollandaise sauce and garnish with a sprinkling of black pepper and chives.

Smoked Haddock Omelette

YES, I KNOW PEOPLE ARE GOING TO SAY IT'S AN OMELETTE ARNOLD BENNETT, but who cares. I made this while filming in Whitby. I got the haddock from a shop called Fortune's, which is famous for smoked kippers mainly, but the haddock was brilliant. I used fresh farm eggs and cream – English, of course – and it was one of the nicest dishes I've ever made.

SERVES 2

300ml (10fl oz) milk
3 bay leaves
2 slices onion
6 black peppercorns
280g (10oz) undyed smoked
   haddock fillet
6 free-range eggs
salt and freshly ground
   black pepper
20g (¾oz) unsalted butter
50ml (2fl oz) double cream
2 tbsp freshly grated Parmesan

1 Mix the milk with 300ml (10fl oz) of water, pour it into a large shallow pan and bring to the boil. Add the bay leaves, onion and peppercorns, and bring back to the boil. Add the smoked haddock, bring back to a simmer and poach for about 3–4 minutes, until the fish is cooked. Lift the fish out on to a plate and leave until cool, then break into flakes, discarding any skin and bones. Preheat the grill to high.

2 Whisk the eggs and season. Heat a 23–25cm (9–10in) nonstick frying pan over a medium heat, then add the butter and swirl it around to coat the base and sides of the pan. Pour in the eggs and, as they start to set, drag the back of a fork over the base of the pan, lifting up little folds of egg to allow the uncooked egg to run underneath.

3 When the omelette is set underneath but still moist on top, sprinkle over the flaked smoked haddock. Pour the cream over, add the Parmesan, and grill the omelette until lightly golden. Slide on to a warmed plate, and serve with a crisp green salad.

Hot Cross Buns

THESE TASTE SO GOOD THAT YOU SHOULDN'T JUST MAKE THEM AT EASTER. They are great, I think, with butter for brekkie, with some fried caramel bananas, or toasted with strawberries and balsamic vinegar, with a dollop of clotted cream. Or better still, just with some good old home-made jam. The almond paste recipe makes far more than you need, but it will be useful, if kept in the fridge, for any other cake making.

MAKES 18

FOR THE BASIC BUN DOUGH
450g (1lb) strong plain flour
1 level tsp each of ground
    cinnamon, nutmeg and
    mixed spice
½ tsp ground mace
½ tsp salt
25g (1oz) fresh yeast
55g (2oz) caster sugar
150ml (5fl oz) milk
100–150ml (3½–5fl oz) boiling
    water
85g (3oz) unsalted butter
1 free-range egg, lightly beaten
85g (3oz) raisins
55g (2oz) candied peel, chopped

FOR THE ALMOND PASTE
225g (8oz) icing sugar
450g (1lb) ground almonds
1 large free-range egg
3–4 tsp lemon juice

FOR THE BUN WASH
a little beaten free-range egg
55g (2oz) caster sugar
5 tbsp water

1 Put the flour, spices and salt into a large warmed mixing bowl. Crumble the yeast into another bowl, add 1 heaped tsp of the sugar and 125g (4½oz) flour from the bowl. Pour the milk into a measuring jug, and make up to 250ml (9fl oz) with boiling water straight from the kettle. Using a wooden spoon, mix this hot liquid into the yeast mixture. Go slowly so as to make as smooth a batter as possible. Leave it in a warm place to rise and froth up – this takes about 20 minutes.

2 Mix the rest of the sugar with the remaining flour, and rub in the butter. Form a well in the centre, and put in the egg and the frothy yeast mixture. Mix to a dough with a wooden spoon. Turn it out on to a floured surface and knead for 10 minutes, adding more flour as required, until the dough is coherent and tacky, but not sticky.

3 Wash and dry the mixing bowl, then grease with buttered paper. Place the dough in it. Cover with a damp cloth, or put the whole thing inside an oiled polythene bag. Leave to rise to double its size. This can take anything from 1–3 hours, depending on the room temperature.

4 Punch down the dough, and knead in the fruit and peel. Roll the dough into a long sausage shape on a floured surface and cut it into 18 discs. Shape into round buns, then place them on baking sheets lined with parchment paper. Leave plenty of room to rise and spread.

5 To make the almond paste, sift the icing sugar and mix it with the almonds. Beat the egg thoroughly in a bowl, then add the lemon juice and the dry ingredients. Use a wooden spoon to beat everything to a firm paste. Knead it on a board or smooth surface, sprinkled with icing sugar. Roll out the almond paste and cut into thin strips.

6 To finish, brush the buns with the beaten egg and lay two strips of almond paste on each bun to form a cross. Leave the buns to prove for about 30 minutes. Preheat the oven to 230°C/450°F/Gas 8. Bake the buns for 10–15 minutes. Meanwhile, boil the sugar and water together until syrupy. Brush over the hot buns when they emerge from the oven.

Orange Whisky Marmalade

ORANGE MARMALADE WAS first made in Dundee in Scotland in about 1770. So this whisky version is actually steeped in tradition.

MAKES 1.4KG (3¼LB)

550g (1¼lb) Seville oranges
juice of 1 lemon
1.3 litres (2¼ pints) water
150ml (5fl oz) whisky
1.1kg (2lb 7oz) granulated sugar

1 To sterilise the jam jars, place them in a large pan and cover with cold water. Bring to the boil and simmer for 10–15 minutes. Remove from the water and leave upside down to dry on a clean cloth.

2 Halve the oranges and, using a spoon, scoop out the insides, leaving the pith behind. Reserve the peel. Place the orange juice, membrane and pips in a food processor and blend. Once the mixture is smooth, pass through a sieve into a large non-reactive or preserving pan.

3 Using a tablespoon, scoop out and discard as much of the pith from the reserved peel as possible, then cut the peel into very thin strips. Add to the juice in the pan, then add the lemon juice, water and whisky. Bring to the boil and simmer for about 1–1½ hours, until the peel is tender and the mixture has reduced by half.

4 Add the sugar and mix over a low heat until it has dissolved. Boil for about 10 minutes, removing any froth on the surface with a spoon.

5 Spoon a little of the marmalade on to a cold plate – it should be like jelly. If it is still runny, cook for a further 5–10 minutes. Leave to cool slightly before filling, sealing and labelling the sterilised jars.

Smoked Bacon Welsh Rarebit

YOU CAN MAKE LOADS OF THIS CHEESE MIXTURE IN ONE GO, and it can sit in the fridge for a week. Then, any time of day or night you fancy a quick snack, it's so easy to use. But serve your rarebit with the tomato and apple chutney on page 137, and it becomes a very serious dish indeed.

There is a famous tearoom in Yorkshire called Betty's, where I used to take my Gran. She would have a soft prawn sandwich because of her teeth; I'd have this – and we'd both sit there watching the world go by. She was a very special woman.

SERVES 4–6

12 slices good streaky bacon
4–6 thin slices white bread

FOR THE RAREBIT
375g (13oz) strong Cheddar cheese
75ml (2½ fl oz) milk
100ml (3½fl oz) double cream
1 free-range egg plus 1 egg yolk
½ tbsp mustard powder
25g (1oz) plain flour
25g (1oz) fresh white breadcrumbs
dash of Worcestershire sauce
dash of Tabasco sauce
salt and freshly ground
   black pepper

1 To make the rarebit, grate the cheese into a pan with the milk and cream, and gently warm until the cheese has melted. Do not boil. Leave to cool slightly. Preheat the grill.

2 Add the egg and egg yolk, mustard, flour, breadcrumbs and a dash of both Worcestershire and Tabasco sauces to the cheese mixture. Season, mix well and allow to cool.

3 Grill the bacon until cooked, then grill the bread on one side only. Place the bread, ungrilled side up, into an ovenproof dish, and top with the bacon. Pour the rarebit mixture over the bacon and bread, return to the grill and allow to colour.

4 Remove from the grill and cool a bit before serving with the tomato chutney on page 137.

WEEKDAY LUNCH

Broccoli and Almond Soup

I MADE THIS SOUP WHILE FILMING IN YORK. It's a nice twist to an old English favourite, almond soup. The vegetables came from a man called John Mannion, who is an old friend of the family. I remember going to his stall in York Market (and his shop nearby) as a kid with my Gran and watching her squeeze all the fruit first before buying them. What's great now is that most of the market stalls are selling a mixture of new fruit and veg with traditional. I wonder what my Gran would have thought of garlic and ginger grown in Yorkshire! Probably nothing, as they were never her thing, but she could make a great broccoli soup, and this is as near as I can get to it.

SERVES 4

25g (1oz) butter
2 garlic cloves, peeled and crushed
1 large white onion, peeled
   and diced
225g (8oz) potato, peeled
   and diced
75ml (2½fl oz) white wine
700ml (1¼ pints) vegetable stock
2 heads broccoli, cut into
   small florets
150ml (5fl oz) double cream
85g (3oz) flaked almonds, toasted
2–3 sprigs fresh parsley,
   finely chopped
salt and freshly ground
   black pepper

1 Heat a large saucepan and add the butter. Once foaming, add the garlic and onion, and sweat without colouring for a few minutes. Next add the potato, white wine and stock. Bring to the boil and simmer for 5 minutes to get the potato cooking.

2 Add the broccoli to the pan and continue to cook for a further 6–8 minutes. Add the cream, half the almonds and all the parsley. Bring to the boil, remove from the heat and allow to cool slightly.

3 Blend in a food processor, then return the liquid to the pan. Bring to the boil and season with salt and pepper to taste.

4 To serve, spoon the soup into bowls or mugs and top with the remaining toasted almonds and/or a little partly whipped double cream.

Chicken and Ham Terrine

THIS IS ONE OF THE DISHES I PUT ON THE MENU at The Bistro on board *Ocean Village*, and I love it. But as with most terrines and pâtés, I think it should be served with fruit chutney or caramelised onions, or something else to break up the taste.

SERVES 10–12

16–20 slices streaky bacon
  (depending on the size
  of the terrine)
300g (10½oz) chicken meat,
  minced
300g (10½oz) shoulder of pork,
  minced
600ml (1 pint) double cream
1 free-range egg, beaten
100ml (3½fl oz) Armagnac
3 tbsp each of chopped fresh
  parsley and chives
2 tbsp chopped fresh tarragon
salt and freshly ground
  black pepper
25g (1oz) butter
2 shallots, peeled and
  finely chopped
300g (10½oz) chicken breast meat,
  cut into 5mm (¼in) strips
225g (8oz) sliced cooked ham
140g (5oz) chicken livers

TO GARNISH
pear chutney (see page 134)
mixed dressed salad leaves

1 First, line a terrine dish measuring 28 x 16 x 6cm (11 x 6½ x 2½in) with streaky bacon, allowing the slices to overlap the mould at the sides by a few inches.

2 Put the chicken and pork into a bowl, and work the mixture with a wooden spatula. Stir in the cream, egg, Armagnac and chopped herbs. Add 2 tsp salt per 1kg (2¼lb) meat, and season with pepper.

3 Heat the butter in a small saucepan and sweat the shallots for 2–3 minutes. Cool and add to the meat mixture.

4 Spread half the mixture over the bottom of the terrine, then make a layer with some of the sliced chicken breast, then some of the sliced ham, and fill with some of the remaining mince mixture. Continue with two or three layers of the ham, mince mixture and chicken breast, with a layer of the chicken livers running though the middle of the terrine. Finally, fold the bacon over the terrine from the sides and either cover with a lid or cover with foil. Preheat the oven to 200°C/400°F/Gas 6.

5 Place the terrine in a roasting tray, and half-fill the tray with warm water. Cook in the oven for 1 hour. Remove from the oven and place a weighted board (maximum weight 500g/18oz) on the terrine to compress it gently until it has cooled completely.

6 Serve in thick slices with pear chutney and dressed salad leaves.

Duck Liver and Basil Pâté

IF YOU CAN'T FIND DUCK LIVERS, USE CHICKEN LIVERS INSTEAD. This is another dish we do at my bistro on board *Ocean Village*, but it's so simple – the chutney brings all the flavours together so well. One other thing you could do, of course, is to serve Melba toast. But I think the last time I made that was at my school 'O' levels.

SERVES 14–16

1kg (2$\frac{1}{4}$lb) organic duck livers, all green and thready bits removed

Cognac

2 garlic cloves, peeled and chopped

handful of fresh basil leaves, lightly chopped, plus 2 whole leaves

salt and freshly ground black pepper

350g (12oz) unsalted butter, softened

FOR THE GARNISH
charred slices of brioche
pear chutney (see page 134)
mixed salad leaves

1 Place the whole livers in a single layer in a suitable dish, and scatter over some Cognac. The brandy should not cover the livers, but they do need to wallow in it for several hours. Turn them over so both sides absorb the alcohol.

2 Add the garlic, chopped basil and seasoning to the livers just before cooking. Gently poach the livers in their brew on top of the stove, turning them over after a couple of minutes. Continue to stew until they are cooked on the outside, but pink within – only another couple of minutes. Do not overcook, or you will end up with a drab brown crumbly result.

3 Tip the contents of the dish straight into your blender with two-thirds of the softened butter, and blend until smooth. Check the seasoning, then scrape into a 1kg (2¼lb) terrine and place in the fridge to cool.

4 When cool, clarify the remaining butter by melting it, then removing all the curd-like sediment (*see page* 138). Pour the clear liquid over the surface of the pâté, place a couple of fresh basil leaves in the centre, and put it into the fridge until set.

5 Serve with slices of charred brioche, with the chutney and salad leaves on the side.

Pizza Margherita

THE PIZZA MAY NOT BE TRADITIONALLY BRITISH, but it's sure up there in our favourite things to eat, so it had to be in the book. I love it with some salami milano and cooked chicken but, whatever your taste, use this as a base and you won't go wrong. You can make the pizzas larger if you wish and, of course, they can be any shape you fancy.

MAKES 4 X 25CM (10IN) PIZZAS

olive oil
3 garlic cloves, peeled and
    finely chopped
1kg (2¼lb) vine-ripened
    tomatoes, skinned, seeded and
    roughly chopped
salt and freshly ground
    black pepper
1 tbsp chopped fresh oregano
500g (18oz) buffalo mozzarella
    cheese, thinly sliced
large handful of basil leaves,
    torn into pieces

FOR THE BASE
550g (1¼lb) strong white flour,
    plus extra for dusting
4 tsp easy-blend yeast
2 tsp salt
450ml (16fl oz) hand-hot water
4 tsp olive oil
4 tbsp polenta or semolina

1 For the base, sift the flour, yeast and salt into a bowl, and make a well in the centre. Add the warm water and olive oil, and mix together to a soft dough. Tip the dough out on to a lightly floured surface and knead for 5 minutes, or until smooth and elastic. Return it to the bowl, cover with clingfilm and leave in a warm place for approximately 1 hour, or until doubled in size.

2 Meanwhile, for the topping, heat 6 tbsp of the oil and cook the garlic in a large, shallow pan. As soon as the garlic starts to sizzle, add the tomatoes and some salt and pepper, and simmer quite vigorously for 7–10 minutes, until reduced to a thickish sauce. Season if necessary.

3 Put a large baking tray into the oven and heat the oven to its highest setting. Knock the air out of the dough and knead it briefly once more on a lightly floured surface. Divide into four pieces, and keep the spare ones covered with clingfilm while you shape the first pizza.

4 Sprinkle a spare baking sheet or a pizza peel with some of the polenta or semolina. Roll the dough out into a disc approximately 25cm (10in) in diameter, lift it on to the baking sheet and reshape it with your fingers into a round. Spread one-quarter of the tomato sauce to within about 2.5cm (1in) of the edge. Sprinkle with some of the oregano, then cover with a quarter of the mozzarella cheese slices.

5 Drizzle with a little olive oil, then open the oven door and quickly slide the pizza off the tray on to the hot baking sheet on the top shelf. Bake for 10 minutes, or until the cheese has melted and the crust is crisp and golden. Repeat the assembling and cooking process with the remaining pieces of dough, cooking individually.

6 To serve, scatter with the basil leaves and serve hot.

Smoked Salmon Mousse with Cucumber

SALMON AND CUCUMBER MAKE A GREAT COMBINATION, whether in a sandwich or on a platter of a whole dressed poached salmon. I think this was one of the dishes I did in my first year at college. It's very 1970s, I suppose, but this is what I used to eat in Berni Inns, followed by a sirloin steak with onion rings, peas and carrots, and a jacket potato. That in turn would be followed by – but only if I sat still while my sister tormented me – jelly and ice-cream with hundreds and thousands on the top.

SERVES 4

200g (7oz) smoked salmon
200g (7oz) cooked salmon,
    skin and bone removed
150ml (5fl oz) double cream
100g (3½oz) cream cheese
juice of 1 lemon
½ tsp creamed horseradish
salt and freshly ground
    black pepper

TO SERVE
½ cucumber, finely sliced

1 Place the two types of salmon in a blender and mix to a paste. Remove from the machine and place in a bowl. Partly whip the cream in a separate bowl.

2 Fold the cream cheese into the salmon mixture. Carefully fold in the lemon juice and horseradish, and finally the cream. Do not over mix, as it will split. Season and transfer to a clean bowl or individual ramekins.

3 Serve with the sliced cucumber, as well as some mixed leaves and thickly sliced brown bread with butter.

Gravadlax with Mustard and Dill Sauce

GRAVADLAX SHOULD NEVER BE CONFUSED WITH SMOKED SALMON; it is made in a very different way indeed. You don't need a smoker as you do for smoked salmon – all you need is time. Trust me, this stuff's worth the wait.

SERVES 6

115g (4oz) coarse rock salt
85g (3oz) caster sugar
1 tbsp white peppercorns, crushed
2 large bunches fresh dill
2 x 900g (2lb) thick salmon fillets,
* skin on, scaled and pin bones*
* removed*

FOR THE MUSTARD AND
DILL SAUCE
2 tbsp Dijon mustard
1 tbsp caster sugar
1 free-range egg yolk
150ml (5fl oz) groundnut oil
1 tbsp white wine vinegar
4 tbsp chopped fresh dill
salt and freshly ground
* black pepper*

1 To make the salmon curing mix, place the salt, sugar and white pepper into a medium-sized bowl. Finely chop most of the dill, add to the salt mixture, and stir to combine.

2 Choose a large, shallow, rectangular dish that will hold the salmon fillets, and line it with clingfilm. Sprinkle a quarter of the curing mixture over the base and top with one of the salmon fillets, skin-side down. Sprinkle over half of the remaining curing mix, and top with the other half of the salmon skin-side up. Sprinkle the remaining curing mixture on top of the fillet and wrap in the clingfilm.

3 Weigh the fish down with some cans or weights on top, to remove any excess liquid or moisture. Place in the fridge, turning the salmon over every 6 hours where possible, for 3–4 days.

4 Before serving the gravadlax, rinse the cure off the fish to remove the salt, and pat dry with kitchen paper. Sprinkle the remaining finely chopped dill over one side of the salmon, then sandwich the two fillets together again. Wrap tightly in clingfilm and chill for 6 hours.

5 To make the sauce, whisk the mustard and sugar together with the egg yolk in a large bowl. Gradually whisk in the oil, making sure the oil is well emulsified. Add the vinegar, the fresh dill and some salt and pepper, and mix well.

6 To serve, cut the gravadlax thinly (gravadlax is traditionally served thicker than smoked salmon). Place three or four good slices on a plate along with a spoonful of the sauce. Serve with rye bread.

Cornish Pasty

YOU CAN FIND ALL SORTS OF FANCY RECIPES FOR CORNISH PASTIES, but the simple ones are the best. This dish was never invented to achieve stars in restaurants. It is what it is: a good gut filler (and even better warm, of course). I have kept this recipe very simple and made it here with ready-made pastry, but you can make your own, of course, if you wish.

SERVES 2

500g (18oz) ready-made
  shortcrust pastry
1 free-range egg, beaten, to glaze

FOR THE FILLING
250g (9oz) rump steak
115g–140g (4–5oz) onions,
  peeled and chopped
85g (3oz) turnip, peeled and
  chopped
225g (8oz) potato, peeled and
  thinly sliced
salt and freshly ground
  black pepper
a pinch of dried thyme

1 To make the filling, remove the fat from the lean meat, and cut the meat into rough cubes. Mix together with the vegetables, salt, pepper and thyme. Preheat the oven to 180°C/350°F/Gas 4.

2 Roll out the pastry and cut it into two large dinner-plate circles. Divide the steak mixture between the two, putting it down the middle. Brush the rim of the pastry with beaten egg. Fold over the pastry, to make a half circle, or bring up the two sides to meet over the top of the filling, and pinch them together into a scalloped crest going right over the top of the pasty. Make two holes on top, so that the steam can escape.

3 Place the pasties on a baking sheet and brush them with beaten egg. Bake for 40 minutes. Serve hot or cold.

Green Pea and Smoked Salmon Risotto

FROZEN OR FRESH, TO BE HONEST PEAS ARE GOOD WHATEVER THEY ARE, as I think they're one of the few vegetables that are great from the freezer. The only thing in this recipe is to watch the seasoning – in particular, the salt – as smoked salmon is quite often salty.

SERVES 4

500ml (18fl oz) fresh fish stock
500ml (18fl oz) fresh chicken
  stock
25g (1oz) butter
1 shallot, peeled and chopped
1 garlic clove, peeled and chopped
250g (9oz) arborio rice
50ml (2fl oz) white wine
100g (3¹/₂oz) mascarpone cheese
225g (8oz) smoked salmon, sliced
  into strips
140g (5oz) frozen peas
100g (3¹/₂oz) Parmesan, freshly
  grated
10g (¹/₄oz) fresh flat-leaf parsley,
  finely chopped
salt and freshly ground
  black pepper
extra virgin olive oil

1 Have the two stocks, mixed, in a pan heating on top of the stove.

2 Melt the butter in a pan, and sweat the shallot and garlic for a few minutes, but don't colour. Add the rice to the pan and seal, stirring to coat it with butter, for about 30 seconds over a low heat.

3 Add the white wine to the pan and cook for a further few seconds, before adding the warm stocks, little by little, while stirring. Simmer for about 12 minutes, remembering to keep adding the stocks a little at a time, not all at once, until the rice is cooked but still has some bite.

4 Mix the mascarpone, salmon, peas and Parmesan into the risotto with the parsley, and season well.

5 To serve, put the risotto in the centre of warm plates. Top with a little extra grated Parmesan, and drizzle with a little extra virgin olive oil.

Mackerel with Gooseberry Cream Sauce

MACKEREL IS SUCH AN UNDERRATED FISH, but it must be eaten as fresh as possible. Just simply grilled, it has a wonderful oily taste, and goes very well with chutneys and sour fruits such as gooseberry. Don't turn the fish over while cooking; it will cook through from one side only, as it is so thin when filleted.

SERVES 4

4 large fresh mackerel, filleted
salt and freshly ground
   black pepper
olive oil
100g (3¹/₂oz) green mixed leaves
   dressed with balsamic vinegar
   and extra virgin olive oil

FOR THE GOOSEBERRY SAUCE
225g (8oz) gooseberries
25g (1oz) butter
150ml (5fl oz) double cream
salt and freshly ground
   black pepper
granulated sugar (optional)

1 To make the sauce, top and tail the gooseberries. Melt the butter in a pan, add the gooseberries, cover them and leave to simmer gently until they are cooked, usually about 30 minutes. Mash them down and mix in the cream and some seasoning to soften their sharpness. Add a little sugar if the gooseberries were very young and green, but the sauce should not be sweet like an apple sauce. Preheat the grill.

2 Season to taste and brush the mackerel with olive oil on both sides. Place on an oven tray, skin-side up, and grill for about 5 minutes to cook through.

3 Place the dressed salad leaves on the serving plates with two fillets of mackerel each and a spoonful of the gooseberry sauce.

Cauliflower Cheese

LOVE IT OR LOATHE IT, THE CAULIFLOWER IS A GREAT VEGETABLE. Chefs love to cook with it, but other people are still divided, probably due to the school dinners we used to have – that dreaded grey stuff that was kept warm for hours in steaming trays with lids on. As you queued up for your pile of mash, sausages, wrinkled peas, tinned carrots and cauli that you could see through, you had to ask for extra gravy to bring it back to life. Overcooked cauliflower still scares me to this day.

SERVES 4

1 large cauliflower, divided
  into florets, or use individual
  baby cauliflowers
salt and freshly ground
  black pepper
butter

FOR THE CHEESE SAUCE
1 clove
1 bay leaf
1 small onion, peeled
600ml (1 pint) milk
25g (1oz) butter
25g (1oz) plain flour
freshly grated nutmeg
150ml (5fl oz) single cream
1 tsp English mustard
250g (9oz) mature Cheddar, grated

1 To make the sauce, first stud the clove through the bay leaf into the onion, and place in a saucepan with the milk. Warm the milk slowly to allow the flavours to impregnate the milk.

2 Melt the butter in a suitable saucepan. Once melted, add the flour and cook on a low heat for a few minutes, stirring from time to time. Add the simmering milk, a ladle at a time, and stir to a smooth sauce. Bring to a simmer and cook for about 8–10 minutes.

3 Remove the onion and season the sauce with salt, pepper and nutmeg. Add the single cream, which will loosen the sauce slightly. Add the mustard and 200g (7oz) of the grated Cheddar. Once completely melted into the sauce, taste again for seasoning and strength. Do not boil. Strain through a sieve.

4 Cook the cauliflower florets in a pan of salted water until just tender, a few minutes. Drain. (The cauliflower can be cooked ahead of time and refreshed in ice water. To reheat, either microwave or plunge back into boiling water. If using baby cauliflower, you could keep it whole, as in the photograph.) Warm a knob of butter in a frying pan and add the florets. These can now be rolled, without colouring, in the butter and seasoned with salt and pepper.

5 To finish, preheat the oven to 200°C/400°F/Gas 6 or preheat the grill. Spoon a little cheese sauce into an ovenproof dish, arrange the cauliflower on top and coat with more of the sauce. Sprinkle the last of the grated Cheddar on top and place in the oven or under the grill to melt and colour for 10–15 minutes.

Wild Garlic Pesto

I MADE THIS RECIPE UP WHILE I WAS IN YORKSHIRE AT MY MUM'S. Loads of wild garlic grows there, and you can smell it as you drive or walk past in the spring. The green leaves look similar to sorrel leaves, and you need to pick them from the plant before it flowers. I have made pesto out of the pungent leaves here, but you can also add them to soups and stews, or cut them up into salads.

SERVES 4

450g (1lb) wild garlic leaves
100ml (3¹/₂fl oz) extra virgin
   olive oil
salt and freshly ground
   black pepper
25g (1oz) Parmesan, freshly grated
juice and finely grated zest of
   1 lemon

1 Wash and dry the garlic leaves. Place in a pestle and mortar, and crush down with the olive oil and some salt and pepper.

2 Finish by adding the Parmesan and the lemon juice and zest. Mix well and season again to taste.

Stilton and Red Onion Salad

THIS IS ANOTHER ONE OF THOSE DISHES I DID IN MY FIRST YEAR AT COLLEGE, and I remember it because it's so simple. So once more, it's very 1970s, I suppose, but then again I did eat it a lot in Berni Inns …. Stilton, to my mind, needs a strong robust flavour to accompany it, and red onion fits the bill for this salad.

SERVES 4 AS A STARTER

4 red onions, peeled
2 tbsp olive oil
2 tbsp groundnut oil
2 tbsp balsamic vinegar
squeeze of lemon juice
salt and freshly ground
   black pepper
10 very thin slices baguette
225–350g (8–12oz) mixed
   green leaves
115g (4oz) Stilton cheese,
   broken into pieces

FOR THE DRESSING
3 tbsp Port
2 tbsp Dijon mustard
2 tbsp red wine vinegar
4 tbsp walnut oil
4 tbsp groundnut oil

1 Cut each onion into six wedges, keeping the root of the onion in place to prevent it falling apart. Bring a pan of water to the simmer, add the cut onions and cook for 2 minutes.

2 Warm together the oils, balsamic vinegar and lemon juice. Drain the onions and add them to the oil/vinegar mix. Remove from the heat, season with some salt and pepper, and leave the onions to marinate at room temperature, turning every so often to ensure an even flavour. The onions will be at their best after an hour or so.

3 Preheat the oven to 200°C/400°F/Gas 6. To make the dressing, boil and reduce the Port by half and allow to cool. Mix the mustard with the red wine vinegar. Whisk together the oils and pour slowly on to the mustard and vinegar mixture, while continuing to whisk vigorously. Once all has been added, whisk in the reduced Port and season with salt and pepper.

4 Crisp up the sliced bread by drizzling with a little extra oil and baking for 5–10 minutes.

5 To serve, separate the red onion wedges, and remove from the marinade. Mix with the green leaves and Stilton. Add some of the red wine/Port dressing to bind. Place on a plate, trickle over some more of the dressing and sit the crispy toasts on top.

Sausage Rolls

WEDDINGS AND FUNERALS are usually where we see the very worst of buffet food. It's a chef's pet hate: those rows on rows of sausage rolls, undercooked vol-au-vents filled with cold prawns and mushrooms, Scotch eggs, pickled eggs, warm ham, undressed salad, overcooked dry chipolatas on sticks, and cheap smoked salmon .... How I hate wedding food. But worst of all are the wedding buffet chefs who don't give a damn …

MAKES 16–20

450g (1lb) sausagemeat
(either from your butcher or use normal sausages and take the meat out of the skins)
1 onion, peeled and finely chopped or grated
finely grated zest of ½ lemon
1 heaped tsp each chopped fresh thyme and sage
salt and freshly ground black pepper
freshly grated nutmeg
225g (8oz) ready-made puff pastry
plain flour
1 free-range egg yolk, mixed with 2 tsp milk

1 Preheat the oven to 200°C/400°F/Gas 6. Mix together the sausagemeat, onion, lemon zest and chopped herbs. Season with the salt, pepper and nutmeg. This can now be refrigerated to firm while the pastry is being rolled.

2 Roll the pastry thinly (2–3mm/about ⅛in thick) on a floured surface, then cut into three long strips approximately 10cm (4in) wide.

3 The sausagemeat can now be moulded, using your hands, into three long sausages, preferably 2.5cm (1in) thick. If the meat is too moist, then dust with flour.

4 Sit each 'sausage' on a pastry strip, 2–3cm (¾–1¼in) from the edge of the pastry. Brush the pastry along the other side, close to the sausage, with the egg yolk and milk mixture. Fold the pastry over the meat, rolling it as you do so. When the pastry meets, leave a small overlap before cutting away any excess. Once rolled all along, lift them carefully, making sure that the seal is on the base when put down. Cut each strip into 5cm (2in) sausage rolls.

5 These can now be transferred to a greased baking sheet. The sausage rolls can be left as they are, or you can make three to four cuts with scissors along the top. Brush each with the remaining egg yolk before baking for 20–30 minutes.

6 Once baked golden and crispy, remove from the oven and serve warm.

Potted Crab

POTTED SHRIMPS ARE FAMILIAR TO MOST OF US, in particular those from Morecambe Bay, which come in small buttered pots and are served with lemon and brown bread and butter (a must for all potted fish for me). Crab makes a nice change, as it's quite difficult to find the small brown shrimps in this country (although your fishmonger can probably get them for you). In France, though, they're all over the place – called grey prawns – and they are eaten like we eat nuts at a bar. Heads and all are chewed and swallowed, they are so good …

FILLS 12 RAMEKINS

400g (14oz) white crab meat
400g (14oz) brown crab meat
400g (14oz) best unsalted butter
good pinch of ground mace
good pinch of freshly grated
   nutmeg
1/3 tsp cayenne pepper
salt and freshly ground
   black pepper
lemon juice

1 Preheat the oven to 150°C/300°F/Gas 2. Put the crab meats into separate bowls. Have ready 12 ramekins.

2 Clarify 225g (8oz) of the butter by melting it gently, then pouring it carefully into another pan, leaving behind the milky, curd-like solids (which you discard). Add the mace, nutmeg and cayenne to the clear butter, then pour the spiced butter into the bowl with the white crab meat. Amalgamate well, and season with salt, pepper and a squeeze of lemon juice to taste.

3 Fill each ramekin with a layer of the buttered white crab meat, followed by a layer of brown meat. Finish with a layer of the white meat. You will just have enough room at the top of the ramekin for a final layer of clarified butter (which you will add after poaching in point 4). Place the ramekins in a roasting tin, pour boiling water to come halfway up the sides, and place in the oven for 25 minutes.

4 Remove from the oven, and leave to cool. Clarify the rest of the butter as above, and pour the clear liquid over the ramekins, rather like sealing wax. Place in the fridge to set.

5 The ramekins should be removed from the fridge before serving. Then slip a slim knife blade all the way around the girth of each ramekin right to the bottom, turn the potted crab out on to the palm of your hand, and put each one, butter-side up, on individual plates.

6 Serve with warm toasted brown bread and dressed salad leaves.

Sweet and Sour Prawns

THIS DISH WILL WORK WITH CHICKEN, TOO: cut the breast into thin strips, then roll in cornflour, blanch in boiling water for a minute or two, drain and make as described below. This will not only cook the chicken a little, but also tenderise it at the same time.

SERVES 4

1½ tbsp groundnut oil
1 tbsp coarsely chopped garlic
2 tsp chopped fresh root ginger
4 spring onions, cut into 2.5cm
  (1in) pieces diagonally
450g (1lb) raw prawns, shelled
  and deveined
115g (4oz) red and green pepper,
  cut into 2.5cm (1in) squares
225g (8oz) canned water
  chestnuts, drained and sliced

FOR THE SAUCE
150ml (5fl oz) chicken stock
2 tbsp rice wine or dry sherry
3 tbsp light soy sauce
2 tsp dark soy sauce
1 tbsp tomato paste
3 tbsp Chinese white rice vinegar
  or cider vinegar
1 tbsp caster sugar
1 tbsp cornflour, blended with
  2 tbsp water

1 Heat a wok over a high heat, then add the oil. When it is very hot and slightly smoking, add the garlic, ginger and spring onions, and stir-fry for a couple of seconds.

2 Add the prawns and stir-fry them for 1 minute. Next add the pepper and water chestnuts, and stir-fry for another 30 seconds.

3 Now add all the sauce ingredients except for the cornflour mixture, then turn the heat down and simmer for 3 minutes.

4 Add the cornflour to thicken the sauce, stir-fry for 2 minutes more, and serve with plain or egg-fried rice.

WEEKDAY DINNER

Trenchers seafood restaurant in Whitby

Pan-fried Cod with Cabbage and Smoked Salmon

'COD AND CABBAGE!' I HEAR YOU CRY. But this works, like most fish, with Savoy cabbage. This is not like the school cabbage that scared you when you were younger. It's trendy, that's what it is. Trendy. The dressing recipe below will make more than you need for this recipe, but it will keep in the fridge for a week or so.

SERVES 4

1 small Savoy cabbage,
   about 175g (6oz)
115g (4oz) smoked salmon
25ml (1fl oz) olive oil
4 x 175–200g (6–7oz) thick cod
   fillet steaks, skin on but no
   bones
salt and freshly ground
   black pepper
55g (2oz) butter

FOR THE MUSTARD DRESSING
4 tsp Dijon mustard
2 tbsp white wine vinegar
8 tbsp walnut oil
8 tbsp groundnut oil

1 For the dressing, whisk the mustard with the vinegar. Mix together the two oils and gradually add to the mustard, whisking all the time. Once everything is thoroughly mixed, season with salt and pepper.

2 Remove the dark outside leaves from the cabbage and cut the rest into quarters. The cabbage can now be cut into 1cm (½in) strips. Cut the slices of smoked salmon into pieces about the same size.

3 Heat a frying pan and add the oil. Season the cod fillets, place in the pan, and add half the butter. Cook the fillets for about 3–4 minutes on either side, depending on their thickness, until cooked through.

4 At the same time, heat a pan and add 2–3 tbsp water and the remaining butter. Once the water and butter are boiling, add the cabbage. Season with salt and pepper, and keep turning in the pan. The cabbage will only take 1–2 minutes and it's best eaten when just becoming tender but still with some texture. Add the smoked salmon to the cabbage, check for seasoning and add 4 tbsp of mustard dressing.

5 To serve, simply spoon the cabbage and smoked salmon at the top of the plates, and finish with the pan-fried cod on the side.

Hot Tea-smoked Trout with New Potatoes and Rocket

I FIRST LEARNED THIS DISH WHILE DOING *READY STEADY COOK*, and I have loved it ever since. It tastes as good now as it did then. I've used trout here, but you could use salmon, chicken or duck (the meat needs to be cooked for a few more minutes than the fish). Oh, and one other thing, Fudge loves it, but it makes his breath smell like he's been smoking ten a day …

SERVES 2

2 fresh trout, each about
* 280–350g (10–12oz), gutted*
* and heads taken off*
olive oil
salt and freshly ground
* black pepper*

FOR THE SMOKING MIXTURE
55g (2oz) demerara sugar
55g (2oz) long-grain rice
10 tea bags (any kind, but not
* herbal), torn open and bags*
* discarded*

TO SERVE
450g (1lb) new potatoes
115g (4oz) wild rocket
2–3 tbsp balsamic vinegar
2 tbsp chopped fresh flat-leaf
* parsley*
55g (2oz) Parmesan, freshly grated

1 To make the smoking mixture, put the sugar, rice and tea-leaves into a bowl and mix together. Line a deep roasting tray with foil and pour the tea mixture into the base. Cover with another layer of foil, then place on the stove to heat up.

2 Once it is smoking a little, add the trout on top of the foil. Drizzle with a little olive oil, making sure the fish sits in the foil. Season with salt and pepper before covering with a tight-fitting lid or another piece of foil, and leave to smoke on the stove-top over a medium heat for 15–20 minutes.

3 While the trout is cooking, wash and boil the new potatoes in plenty of salted boiling water for 12–15 minutes, depending on size, until cooked.

4 To dress the salad, simply place the rocket in a bowl with the balsamic vinegar, 6 tbsp olive oil and a pinch each of salt and black pepper, and toss.

5 To serve, drain the hot new potatoes and place them in a bowl with the parsley. Finish the salad with the Parmesan and place on the plate, with the hot smoked trout on the side.

Crab Risotto

THIS IS ONE OF MY FAVOURITE recipes in the book – it just tastes so good.

SERVES 4

*300ml (10fl oz) fresh chicken
   stock*
300ml (10fl oz) fresh fish stock
*2 garlic cloves, peeled and
   finely chopped*
*2 shallots, peeled and
   finely chopped*
25g (1oz) butter
280g (10oz) arborio rice
100ml (3½fl oz) white Muscat wine
*2 green chillies, seeded and
   chopped*
pinch of curry powder
½ tbsp Thai green curry paste
1 stick lemongrass, crushed
3 kaffir lime leaves
2 tbsp mascarpone cheese
50ml (2fl oz) double cream
*15g (½oz) each of fresh flat-leaf
   parsley and coriander, finely
   chopped*
*450g (1lb) fresh white and dark
   crab meat*
*115g (4oz) Parmesan, freshly
   grated, plus extra for serving*
juice of 1 lime
*salt and freshly ground
   black pepper*
chilli oil

1 Heat the two stocks, mixed, in a pan on top of the stove. Meanwhile, sweat the garlic and shallots in the butter for about a minute. Add the rice, then the wine, with the green chillies, curry powder, curry paste, lemongrass and lime leaves. Stir to coat the rice with fat.

2 Add the warm stock, a ladle at a time, while simmering and stirring. Stir, and keep adding stock, until the rice is cooked, which should take about 13–15 minutes.

3 Once the rice is cooked but still with a little bite, add the mascarpone, cream, chopped herbs, crab meat and Parmesan. Adjust with more stock and cream if need be, then add the lime juice and season well.

4 Place the risotto in the centre of the plates and top with a little chilli oil and some extra Parmesan.

Pan-fried Calf's Liver with Bacon and Onions

I LIKE CALF'S LIVER, but what I really remember is the tripe and onions I had when I was a kid. It's hard to find now. There is one place that still does good tripe and onions, and that's a café in Leeds city centre vegetable market. It tastes great, but it's even better as the café where it's served is full of old blokes telling stories of the old days. A fab place.

SERVES 4

8 medium onions, peeled and
  sliced
85g (3oz) butter
8 rashers smoked streaky bacon
100ml (3½fl oz) Madeira, plus
  extra for deglazing
900ml (1½ pints) beef or
  chicken stock
675g (1½lb) calf's liver, thinly
  sliced
salt and freshly ground
  black pepper

TO SERVE
mashed potatoes (see page 61)

1 Preheat the grill to high. Sauté the onions in 25g (1oz) of the butter until well caramelised. This will take about 15 minutes. While the onions are cooking, crisp the bacon under the grill.

2 Once the onion is ready, add the Madeira and stock and reduce by half, until you have a rich sauce. Check the seasoning and leave to one side.

3 Heat a frying pan on a high heat and add a knob of the remaining butter. Cook the liver in batches to keep the pan really hot. Season while in the pan. The liver will only take about 1–2 minutes to cook on each side, and should be nice and pink in the middle.

4 Remove the liver from the pan and deglaze the pan with a little more Madeira, then add the reduced onion sauce as well, and season.

5 To serve, place the mashed potatoes on the plate, top with the liver and spoon over the sauce. Top with the crispy bacon.

Rib-eye Steak with Caesar Salad

RIB-EYE STEAK HAS ONLY REALLY BECOME POPULAR OVER THE PAST 10 YEARS, but it is such a great piece of meat. It comes from the end of the sirloin part of the beef which the rib joint is attached to (where you get the rib joint for roasting from). I love steak and salad, and Caesar salad works particularly well in this case. The recipe for the dressing was invented by a chef I used to work with – cheers, Adam!

SERVES 4

4 rib-eye steaks, about 225g (8oz)
salt and freshly ground
    black pepper
olive oil

FOR THE CAESAR SALAD
2 Cos lettuces
2 thick slices white bloomer,
    cubed
about 25g (1oz) butter
4 garlic cloves
150ml (5fl oz) white wine
4 free-range egg yolks
2 anchovy fillets
140g (5oz) Parmesan, freshly
    grated
300ml (10fl oz) vegetable oil
1 tbsp Dijon mustard

1 To start the salad, separate the lettuce leaves, and wash and dry well, then tear into chunky pieces. Place in a serving bowl. Gently cook the bread cubes in the butter in a frying pan until golden brown.

2 To start the Caesar dressing, peel the garlic and place in a pan with the wine. Bring to the boil and cook for about 5 minutes, until the cloves are soft. Using a hand blender, blend the wine and garlic together with the egg yolks, anchovy fillets and cheese, adding the oil slowly to stop the mix from splitting. This shouldn't happen, as the cheese should make the mix blend together more easily. Add the mustard and seasoning to taste.

3 Preheat a frying pan on the stove. Season the steaks with salt and pepper, and cook in a little olive oil. If you want medium, this should take about 3–4 minutes on both sides. Once cooked, remove the steaks from the pan and place them on the plate while you sort out the salad.

4 To serve, throw the bread cubes into the bowl with the lettuce, add the dressing, and mix together well. Season and munch away.

Meatballs with Tomato Sauce

A GROWN-UP VERSION OF A KID'S DELIGHT. I remember hating meatballs as a child, as my Nana used to cook them all the time, but they were truly awful, always from a tin and never heated through, and served with a mound of overcooked rice. My sister and I used to be made to sit through this ordeal, and we weren't allowed to leave the table until we had finished. I used to hide mine, anywhere and everywhere I could …

SERVES 4

2 shallots, peeled and chopped
1 garlic clove, peeled and chopped
olive oil
450g (1lb) tail of beef fillet
2 tsp Dijon mustard
splash of Worcestershire sauce
50ml (2fl oz) double cream
salt and freshly ground
  black pepper

FOR THE BASIC TOMATO SAUCE
1.5kg (3lb 5oz) ripe and meaty
  tomatoes
4 tbsp olive oil
1 medium onion, peeled and very
  finely sliced
1 garlic clove, peeled and coarsely
  chopped
1 tbsp chopped fresh oregano
10 small fresh basil leaves,
  shredded

1 For the tomato sauce, plunge the tomatoes into boiling water for 1 minute to loosen the skin. Remove the skin, and cut the tomatoes in half. Discard the inner liquid and seeds, leaving only the flesh, which you coarsely chop.

2 Heat the oil in a pan and fry the onion for 5 minutes. Add the garlic and fry for a further minute. Add the tomatoes and bring to the boil, then add the oregano, reduce the heat and simmer for 30–40 minutes. Halfway through, add the basil leaves.

3 When the sauce has finished cooking, add some salt to taste, and liquidise. Keep warm. (It keeps for a few days in the fridge, but is best if eaten when freshly made.)

4 Meanwhile, to make the meatballs, sauté the shallots and garlic quickly in a little oil to take off the rawness, then allow to cool. Mince the beef through the fine plate of a mincer into a bowl. Add the shallots, garlic, mustard, Worcestershire sauce and cream. Beat well together, then season to taste with salt and pepper.

5 Using a little oil on your hands, shape the mixture into 8–10 even-sized shapes about the size of a golf ball. Leave for 10 minutes, covered, in the fridge to firm up.

6 Preheat a pan on the stove and add a little olive oil. Fry the meatballs until golden brown all over, and serve with the warm tomato sauce.

Beef and Black Sheep Ale Pie

MASHAM, PRONOUNCED 'MASS-EM', which is just off the A1 near Thirsk, has two breweries, Theakstons and the Black Sheep Brewery. It was once also home to one of the largest sheep markets in the country, which was held in the town's large market square. Sadly that trade has now gone, but the breweries are still going strong. Run by Paul Theakston – yes, Theakston – the Black Sheep Brewery is open to the public; it has a shop and bistro, offers tours around the brewery itself, and is well worth a visit. They produce several beers of various strengths, the strongest being Riggwelter; the words 'rigged' and 'welted' in old Yorkshire slang would suggest to a farmer that one of his sheep is upside down. Trust me, a few pints of this stuff, and you'd be rigged, but it's the best beer I have tasted in a long time.

SERVES 4

900g (2lb) stewing beef, diced
25g (1oz) plain flour
salt and freshly ground
    black pepper
butter
2 white onions, peeled and sliced
2 garlic cloves, peeled and sliced
2 medium carrots, peeled and
    sliced
140g (5oz) button mushrooms,
    wiped
2 sprigs fresh thyme
1 bay leaf
400ml (14fl oz) Black Sheep Ale
500ml (18fl oz) fresh beef stock
1 free-range egg, beaten, for egg
    wash
300g (10½oz) ready-rolled puff
    pastry

1 Preheat the oven to 180°C/350°F/Gas 4, and place a large casserole dish on a medium heat on the stove.

2 While the dish is heating, place the meat in a bowl, and add the flour and seasoning, turning to coat. When the pan is hot, melt about 15g (½oz) of the butter. Add the meat in batches, adding more butter if necessary, and seal until golden brown.

3 Once browned, add the vegetables, herbs and liquids to the meat, and bring to a simmer on the stove. Cover with a lid or some foil, and either gently simmer on top of the stove for 1½ hours or (what I would do) cook it in the oven for 1¼ hours. Once the meat is tender, season and tip into an ovenproof oven-to-table pie dish. Increase the oven temperature to 200°C/400°F/Gas 6.

4 Brush the beaten egg along the edges of the dish and top with the puff pastry. Pinch the edges of the dish so that the pastry will stick to it, and trim off any remaining pieces of pastry from around the edge. Use the pastry trimmings to make leaves, berries and a decorative rope to go along the outside. Make holes in the top for steam to escape. Brush the pastry all over with the remaining egg wash, and place the pie dish on a baking tray.

5 Bake for 30–40 minutes, until the pastry is golden brown on the top. (Use the baking tray, as the mixture inside can sometimes bubble out and make one hell of a mess on the bottom of your cooker.)

Cottage Pie

WHY IS THIS ALWAYS MIXED UP WITH SHEPHERD'S PIE? Think about it: how many shepherds do you see looking after beef cattle ...

SERVES 4–6

675g (1½lb) minced beef
salt and freshly ground
    black pepper
25ml (1fl oz) olive oil
butter
3 onions, peeled and finely
    chopped
3 carrots, peeled and cut into 1cm
    (½in) dice
4 celery sticks, cut into 1cm
    (½in) dice
½ tsp ground cinnamon
½ tsp chopped fresh rosemary
1 tbsp tomato purée
1 tbsp tomato ketchup
2 tsp Worcestershire sauce
150ml (5fl oz) red wine
25g (1oz) plain flour
200ml (7fl oz) beef stock
900g (2lb) mashed potatoes
    (see page 61)

1 Season the minced beef with salt and pepper, and pan-fry in the oil in a hot frying pan. For the best results, fry in batches. As one lot is fried and coloured, pour off from the pan and drain in a colander.

2 In another large saucepan, melt a knob of butter. Add the vegetables and season with salt, pepper and cinnamon, then add the rosemary. Cook for 5–6 minutes, until beginning to soften. Add the mince, tomato purée, ketchup and Worcestershire sauce, and stir into the mix. Add the red wine in three parts and turn the heat up, reducing each time. Sprinkle the flour into the pan and cook for 2–3 minutes.

3 Pour in the beef stock, bring to a soft simmer, cover and gently cook for about 1–1½ hours on top of the stove. During the cooking time, the sauce may become too thick; if so, add a little water to loosen. However, remember that the mash will spread on top, so don't allow the sauce to become too thin.

4 During the last 30 minutes of the cooking time, the mashed potatoes can be made. Reduce the quantities of the butter and cream or milk given in the recipe on page 61, to give a slightly firmer topping.

5 Once the cottage pie mince is ready, spoon into a suitable ovenproof serving dish. The mashed potatoes can now be spooned or piped on top, brushed with a little butter and finished in a very hot oven or under the grill to become golden. Another method is to allow the mince to become cold in the dish before covering with the potato. This can now be refrigerated until needed, then reheated at 200°C/400°F/Gas 6 for 35–40 minutes.

Steak, Guinness and Oyster Pie

I WAS FILMING A SERIES FOR UK FOOD AROUND BRITAIN on a big yacht (as ya do), and came across the town of Whitstable. What a fab place for seafood: the oysters here were fantastic.

SERVES 6

900g (2lb) braising steak,
   such as blade or chuck,
   cut into 4–5cm (1½–2in) chunks
salt and freshly ground
   black pepper
25g (1oz) plain flour
5 tbsp sunflower oil
25g (1oz) unsalted butter
225g (8oz) small button
   mushrooms, trimmed
2 onions, peeled and thinly sliced
½ tsp caster sugar
300ml (10fl oz) Guinness
300ml (10fl oz) fresh beef stock
   (one of the ready-made pots
   will do)
3 sprigs fresh thyme
2 bay leaves
2 tbsp Worcestershire sauce
12 Pacific oysters
500g (18oz) chilled ready-made
   puff pastry
1 free-range egg, beaten, for
   brushing

1 Season the steak, then toss with the flour and shake off, but reserve the excess. Heat 3 tbsp of the oil in a large saucepan, and brown the meat in two batches until well coloured. Transfer to a plate. Add another tbsp of the oil, half the butter and the mushrooms to the pan and fry briefly. Set aside with the beef. Add the rest of the oil and butter, the onions and sugar to the pan, and fry over a medium-high heat for 20 minutes, until browned. Stir in the reserved flour, Guinness and stock, and bring to the boil, stirring.

2 Return the beef and mushrooms to the pan with the thyme, bay leaves, Worcestershire sauce and a little seasoning. Cover and simmer for 1½ hours, until the meat is just tender. Lift the meat, mushrooms and onions out of the liquid and put into a deep pie dish. Boil the liquid until reduced by half. Remove and discard the herbs, season and pour into the dish. Stir well and leave to cool.

3 To open the oysters, wrap one hand in a tea towel and hold an oyster in it with the flat shell uppermost. Push the point of an oyster knife into the hinge, and wiggle the knife until the hinge breaks and you can slide the knife between the two shells. Twist the point of the knife upwards to lever up the top shell, cut through the point of the ligament and lift off the top shell. Release the oyster from the shell. Add to the dish and push down into the sauce. Push a pie funnel into the centre.

4 Preheat the oven to 200°C/400°F/Gas 6. Roll out the pastry on a lightly floured surface until 2.5cm (1in) larger than the top of the pie dish. Cut off a thin strip from around the edge, brush with egg and press on to the rim of the dish. Brush with more egg, cut a small cross into the centre of the pastry lid and lay over the dish. Press the edges together to seal. Trim any excess and crimp the edges. Chill for 20 minutes. Brush the top of the pie with beaten egg and bake for 30–35 minutes until the pastry is crisp and golden and the filling is bubbling hot.

Egg and Bacon Salad

HERE IS AN EASY SALAD THAT CAN BE SERVED ON ITS OWN OR AS A STARTER. You can, of course, poach the eggs as a change, or use pancetta instead of streaky bacon. When doing the latter, though, crisp up the pancetta on an oven tray. This will stop the pancetta sticking to the grill tray while cooking.

SERVES 4

4 slices thick-sliced white bread,
  crusts removed
4 soft-boiled free-range eggs
  (boiled from room temperature
  for 5 minutes in simmering water)
6 rashers thick-sliced back or
  streaky bacon
4 little gem lettuces, leaves
  separated, rinsed and drained
salt and freshly ground
  black pepper
4 spring onions, washed and finely
  shredded
3 tbsp red wine vinegar
2 tbsp each of olive and
  groundnut oil, mixed

1 Cut the slices of bread into 1cm (½in) dice. Shell the boiled eggs, and cut into quarters.

2 The bacon can now be pan-fried until crispy in a nonstick pan with no oil. Any fat content will be released into the pan from the bacon. This will also happen if grilling. Whichever method you choose, keep the bacon fat for frying the bread. Once cooked, remove the bacon from the pan and keep warm.

3 Add the bread dice to the bacon fat, and fry until golden and crispy. You might need a little extra oil to achieve a golden colour.

4 Season the salad leaves with salt and pepper. It's best, whenever making salads, to sprinkle salt around the bowl and not directly on to the leaves. This prevents the salt from falling on to wet leaves and sticking in lumps.

5 Chop the bacon into chunky strips, and mix into the leaves with the spring onions and fried bread. Mix together the red wine vinegar and the oils. This can be spooned over the leaves, adding just enough to coat.

6 Arrange in a large bowl as one large salad. The soft-boiled egg quarters can now also be seasoned with salt and pepper and placed among the leaves. Serve.

Cumberland Sausage

KIDS LOVE TO MAKE THIS RECIPE AS IT'S GREAT FUN TO DO. It's even better if you can buy a sausage-making machine (they're not too expensive – sometimes under £50). If you can't find one, you can use a piping bag, although it's harder work. Get sausage skins – at least 60cm (2 feet) in length – from your local butcher; you can find synthetic ones now as well.

SERVES 4–6

*450g (1lb) boned, skinned
   shoulder of pork*
175g (6oz) hard back pork fat
4 rashers smoked bacon
*1 tsp each of grated nutmeg
   and mace*
*25g (1oz) white breadcrumbs,
   soaked in 8 tbsp hot water*
*salt and freshly ground
   black pepper*

1 Cut the pork, fat and bacon into strips, and put first through the coarse blade of the mincing machine, then through the medium blade. Add the spices, then the soaked, squeezed breadcrumbs. Mix well together with your hands, then add salt and plenty of pepper.

2 Rinse the salt from the sausage skins. Ease one end of a piece of skin on to the cold tap. Run cold water gently through the skin, to make sure there are no splits or large holes. Turn off the tap, remove the skin and ease it on to the long spout of the sausage-making attachment. Screw the whole thing on to the mincing machine with a coarse blade in position.

3 Feed the pork sausage meat through the mincer again and, as it comes through, slide the skin gently off the attachment and coil it on to a large plate. Leave in the fridge until next day, then bake the whole coil – enough for four on its own, or six as part of a meal. When ready to cook, preheat the oven to 180°C/350°F/Gas 4.

4 Cook the coil for 30–45 minutes in the oven, pricking it before putting into the oven on a greased tray. Or you could fry the coil in a pan on top of the stove, in a little oil – but the oven is easier.

The Best Cheeseburger

THIS ONE DISH HAS CHANGED THE WAY WE EAT more than any other food in the world. Everybody loves burgers, from burnt to a cinder by the old man who once a year takes over the cooking on the barbecue, to the 'drive-thru' eaten from in-between your legs as you drive off to the next meeting. But there's one thing that gets me going, and it's those pretentious chefs who slag off burgers in favour of fillet steak.

SERVES 4

2 shallots, peeled and chopped
splash of olive oil
675g (1½lb) tail of beef fillet
4 tbsp chopped gherkins
2 tbsp double cream
½ tsp Dijon mustard
splash of Worcestershire sauce
salt and freshly ground
  black pepper
1 ball mozzarella cheese, drained
  and cut into 4 slices

1 Sauté the chopped shallots quickly in the oil to take off the rawness, then allow to cool.

2 Mince the fillet of beef into a bowl through the fine plate of a mincer. Add the shallots, gherkins, cream, mustard and Worcestershire sauce. Beat well together and season to taste with salt and pepper.

3 Using a little oil on your hands, shape the mixture into four even-sized burger shapes. Then, using the palm of your other hand, mould the burger into a bowl shape and place a slice of the mozzarella in the middle. Fold over the meat to enclose it, then reshape into a burger. Leave in the fridge to firm up for at least 30 minutes.

4 Preheat the grill, then cook the burgers medium-rare, about 4 minutes on each side. Season well.

Mashed Potatoes

HOW GOOD DOES GOOD MASHED POTATO TASTE? I'll tell you how good – it tastes fantastic. It goes with anything: it can top fish pies or it can simply be served with sausages and onion gravy. I could eat this just with cold roast lamb – that's my favourite.

SERVES 4

900g (2lb) large Maris Piper
*   potatoes, peeled and quartered*
115g (4oz) unsalted butter
125ml (4fl oz) single cream
salt and freshly ground
*   black pepper*
freshly grated nutmeg

1 Boil the potatoes in salted water until cooked, about 20–25 minutes, depending on size.

2 Drain off all the water, replace the lid and shake the pan vigorously, which will start to break up the boiled potatoes. Add the butter and single cream, a little at a time, while mashing the potatoes.

3 Season with salt, pepper and some nutmeg according to taste. The potatoes will now be light, fluffy, creamy and ready to eat.

Chips and French Fries

NOTHING CAN BEAT CHIPS – whether fat or thin – with a little salt and ketchup.

SERVES 4–6

vegetable oil, for deep-frying
4–6 large potatoes, about
  1.5kg (3lb 5oz)
salt

1 Heat the oil in a deep-fat fryer or a deep, heavy-based pan to 95°C/200°F for blanching.

2 For good large chips, peel then trim the potatoes into rectangles. Now cut into 1cm (½in) thick slices, then cut again to give chips 1cm (½in) wide. If you want French fries, then simply halve the thickness, making them 5mm x 6–7.5cm (¼ x 2½–3in).

3 The chips now need to be blanched in the preheated fryer. This is very important, as it guarantees the chips will be totally cooked before serving. Frying them at 95°C/200°F will cook them without allowing them to colour. The large chips will take up to 10 minutes before becoming tender; the smaller fries will need only 6–8 minutes.

4 Once cooked, check with a knife. When ready, remove from the oil and drain. The chips or fries can be left to cool on greaseproof paper and even chilled before finishing in the hot fryer.

5 To finish, preheat the oil in the fryer to 180°C/350°F. Once hot, place the chips in the fat. These will now take around 2–3 minutes to become golden brown and crispy. Shake off any excess fat and sprinkle with salt before serving.

Simple Lamb Curry

WHEN I WAS FILMING IN AN INDIAN RESTAURANT IN BIRMINGHAM, this tasted so good I just had to get the recipe. The chef wouldn't cooperate at first but, after a night on the town and many beers, I got it in the end. At a cost, I might add, as my headache was unreal the day after.

SERVES 4

2 tbsp vegetable oil

900g (2lb) boneless, rolled shoulder of lamb, trimmed and cut into 3cm (1¼in) cubes

2 onions, peeled and roughly chopped

4 garlic cloves, peeled and crushed

1 tbsp grated fresh root ginger

1 tbsp ground turmeric

1½ tbsp garam masala

1½ tbsp ground cumin

1 tbsp chilli powder

1 tbsp plain flour

6 large tomatoes, chopped

1 x 400g can coconut milk

600ml (1 pint) chicken stock

250g (9oz) baby spinach leaves, stalks removed

200g (7oz) plain yoghurt

salt and freshly ground black pepper

1 Heat 1 tbsp of the oil in a large pan, add the lamb and cook over a high heat to brown it quickly all over. Remove the lamb from the pan, place in a bowl and leave to one side.

2 Add the remaining oil to the pan, together with the onions, garlic and ginger, and cook gently for a few minutes until softened and golden brown. Add the spices and cook for a minute, then add the flour and mix well.

3 Add the tomatoes and coconut milk, and return the lamb to the pan. Add just enough of the chicken stock to cover the meat, and stir to release all the bits from the bottom of the pan. Cover and simmer gently for about 1 hour, until the lamb is tender, stirring occasionally.

4 Skim any excess fat off the surface. Stir in the spinach and cook for a few minutes until just wilted, then stir in the yoghurt and season. Serve with plain boiled basmati rice.

SUNDAY LUNCH

Jonathan Cooper at Bond Hill Pigs in Scarborough

Whole Poached Salmon

MY MOTHER USED TO DO THIS FOR DINNER PARTIES AT HOME IN THE 1980S, served with lemon and sliced cucumber. If this dish could speak, it would say 'summer is here'. With buttered Jersey Royal potatoes, green salad and a glass of white wine, it's fantastic.

SERVES 8–10

1 whole salmon,
    about 2.5–2.75kg (5^1/$_2$–6lb)
2 bay leaves
1 onion, peeled and chopped
4 tbsp white wine vinegar
1 lemon, quartered, plus extra, cut
    into wedges, to serve
salt and coarsely ground
    black pepper
mayonnaise, to serve

1 Place the salmon in a fish kettle or, if you're like me, in a large roasting tin. (I never think it's worth spending £50 on something you use only a few times, and can't even fit in the cupboard.)

2 Pour in enough cold water to cover the fish (it must be covered). Add the bay leaves, onion, vinegar, lemon quarters, and a good pinch of salt and a little black pepper.

3 Cover with a lid, and bring to the boil on top of the stove. It is easier and quicker to put two rings on underneath the fish. Once it is boiling, turn off the heat and allow the fish to stand in the water until cool.

4 Carefully remove the salmon and place on a board. Scrape off the skin, and place on a large flat serving dish. Serve with the extra lemon wedges and a bowl of mayonnaise.

Stuffed Seabass with Onions and Honey

I GO FISHING WITH MY MATES Steve and Jo, and a fisherman, Rick, from Poole harbour about once a month. First, we go out and catch sand eels (they're small sardine-like fish), then we use these and live mackerel to catch the bass while drifting over ledges just off the Isle of Wight Needles. Not only is it a great day of beer, packet sarnies and chocolate bars, but also the catch is the best fish I have ever eaten. Simply cooked, fresh fish is one of the true pleasures of life, but catching your own makes the experience a little more special.

SERVES 4

3 large white onions, peeled
* and sliced*
2 garlic cloves, peeled and crushed
olive oil
dash of white wine vinegar
3 tbsp runny honey
salt and freshly ground
* black pepper*
4 small seabass, about 500g
* (18oz) each in weight, scaled*
* and gutted*
1 sprig fresh thyme
2 bay leaves
1 sprig fresh rosemary

1 Preheat the oven to 200°C/400°F/Gas 6. Fry the onions and garlic in a little oil in a hot pan. Add the white wine vinegar and honey, and cook until golden brown. Season and allow to cool.

2 Place the fish on an oven tray, and score the skin on top two or three times with a knife. Stuff the cavity with the onion mixture and herbs.

3 Season with salt and pepper, drizzle with olive oil, and roast in the oven for about 15 minutes.

4 Remove from the oven, and serve whole with the juices from the tray poured over the top, with a dressed salad.

Seabass with Mango Chutney and Red Pepper Essence

THIS IS ANOTHER GREAT BASS RECIPE I make with the catch we get from our fishing trips. Bass was always deemed an expensive fish in the past, but due to farming the price has come down. This fish remains the king of the sea, though, and will always make me look forward to another day out on the boat fishing.

SERVES 4

4 x 125g (4^1/$_2$oz) seabass fillets, bones removed, but skin on
olive oil
butter
115g (4oz) beansprouts
juice of 1 lime
2 tbsp sesame oil
a small bunch of fresh coriander, chopped
8 tbsp smooth mango chutney

FOR THE RED PEPPER ESSENCE
6 red peppers, stalk and seeds removed, chopped
100ml (3^1/$_2$fl oz) cold water

1 Make the red pepper essence by placing the red peppers and water in a liquidiser and processing for 2 minutes. Tip into a clean tea towel placed over a bowl, and squeeze out the liquid. Tip this into a pan and reduce over the heat by three-quarters, until it resembles runny honey in texture. Allow to cool.

2 Pan-fry the seabass, skin-side down, in a little olive oil and butter. When the skin is crisp and brown, turn the fish over and turn off the heat.

3 Dress the beansprouts in the lime juice and sesame oil, and scatter the coriander over them.

4 Warm the mango chutney and spoon into the centre of each serving plate. Top with the beansprouts and fish, drizzle the pepper essence around the edge and serve.

Seared Halibut with Mussels and Onion Sauce

HALIBUT IS A LARGE, SOMETIMES MASSIVE, FLAT FISH that is expensive because chefs love to place it on their menus. It's important that you don't overcook it, as it will become dry. The flavours of the sauce may appear strong, but halibut is a meaty fish like salmon and monkfish, and can take it. Use mussel meat if you want, as it saves a load of hassle, but I think a few mussels left in their shells look good.

SERVES 4

4 x 175g (6oz) halibut fillets
1 tbsp olive oil
25g (1oz) butter
salt and freshly ground
 black pepper

FOR THE ONION SAUCE
1.5kg (3lb 5oz) fresh mussels,
 beards removed, or 85g (3oz)
 mussel meat
2 tsp fresh chopped thyme
1 bay leaf
250ml (9fl oz) muscat wine
25g (1oz) butter
2 onions, peeled and finely sliced
1 small leek, finely diced
½ fennel bulb, sliced
200g (7oz) brown chestnut
 mushrooms, sliced
pinch of curry powder
25ml (1fl oz) Pernod
100ml (3½fl oz) double cream
40g (1½oz) fresh flat-leaf parsley
pinch of saffron strands

1 Discard any mussels that gape or do not close when tapped on the sink – they are probably dead. Heat a large saucepan until very hot. Add the mussels, thyme, bay leaf and one-third of the wine. Cover and heat for a minute or two, then shake the pan well.

2 Continue to cook for a minute or two, then remove the lid. When the mussels have all opened, drain over a bowl to save the cooking liquid. Discard any mussels that are still closed, and the bay leaf. Remove some or all of the mussels from their shells, and discard the shells.

3 In the same saucepan, melt a little of the butter and caramelise the onions. Cook gently until the onions are soft and brown in colour, about 10 minutes. Add the leek, fennel, mushrooms, curry powder and Pernod. Cover the pan and gently sweat the vegetables for about 7 minutes, or until softened but not coloured. Add the remaining wine and bring to the boil. Cook, uncovered, until the cooking liquid has almost completely evaporated. Add the reserved mussel liquor, and cook, uncovered, for 5 minutes to reduce again.

4 In a nonstick pan, heat the olive oil and butter for the fish. Season the halibut and place in the hot pan. Cook for 3–4 minutes before turning over to get some nice colour on the flesh.

5 Meanwhile, add the cream and parsley to the sauce and bring back to the boil. Sprinkle in the saffron, heat for 1–2 minutes and season to taste. Mix the mussels in and season.

6 Divide the sauce between four warm plates, and serve with the halibut on the top, and a few mussels in their shells to decorate.

Roast Pork and Roast Potatoes

EVEN COLD ROAST PORK WITH COLD APPLE SAUCE IS FANTASTIC, let alone straight from the oven just roasted. How many of you are always tempted to taste a thick slice while you're carving? All, if you're like me, and you can't resist the caramelised bit on the end. And I can never walk past one of those hog roasts without grabbing a floury bun filled with sliced meat and Paxo stuffing. Delicious!

SERVES 6

1 x 1.8kg (4lb) boned and rolled
shoulder or loin of pork
salt and freshly ground
black pepper
bones from the joint (optional)
10 medium King Edwards, Desirée
or Maris Piper potatoes, peeled
and halved
sunflower oil
1–2 tsp Marmite
100ml (3½fl oz) red wine
250ml (9fl oz) gravy, made
from gravy granules
1 tsp cornflour mixed with
a little cold water

1 Put your joint of pork on a rack set over a dish or small roasting tin, and leave it somewhere cool and airy for a few hours, so the skin can dry off. Preheat your oven to the highest possible setting.

2 Season the cut faces of the pork with salt and pepper, but leave the skin untouched. Place the pork skin-side up in a large roasting tin – on the bones, if you have them. Roast for 20 minutes, then lower the oven temperature to 180°C/350°F/Gas 4, and continue to roast for 30 minutes per 450g (1lb) – so a 1.8kg (4lb) joint will take a further 2 hours – basting every 15 minutes or so.

3 To make the roast potatoes, simmer the potatoes in water for 3–4 minutes, then drain, reserving the cooking water for the gravy. Add them to the roasting tin, along with about 6 tbsp oil, about 1½ hours before the pork will be ready. Turn them over once or twice until well coated in the oil. Roast alongside the pork, turning them a couple of times during cooking.

4 Remove the pork from the oven, transfer to a tray and leave to rest. If the potatoes are not quite brown enough, transfer them to a small roasting tin and return to the oven whilst the pork is resting.

5 For the gravy, pour off the excess fat from the roasting tin and put the tin over a medium heat. Add 600ml (1 pint) of the reserved cooking water and scrape the base of the tin with a wooden spoon to loosen all the caramelised juices. Add the Marmite, red wine and liquid gravy. Bring to the boil, and boil for a few minutes. Thicken with the cornflour (you may not need it all – just enough to get a good consistency). Strain into a warmed sauceboat, and adjust the seasoning if necessary.

6 To carve, cut and remove the strings. Slide a knife under the crackling, lift it off and break it into pieces. Carve the pork across into thin slices, and arrange them on a warmed serving plate with the crackling and roast potatoes. Serve with the gravy and some vegetables.

Roast Parsnips

I NEVER REALLY LIKED THESE WHEN I WAS YOUNG, and I feel I missed out on them then, as I used to watch my Dad munch on them hot and cold. Sorry, Mum, for not eating them as a kid, but I love 'em now.

SERVES 6

900g (2lb) parsnips, peeled
    and quartered (or, if small and
    don't need to be quartered,
    then 750g/1lb 10oz should
    be enough)
2 tbsp olive oil
2 sprigs fresh thyme, leaves
    picked from the stalks
salt and freshly ground
    black pepper
40g (1¹/₂oz) butter
4–6 tbsp runny honey

1 Preheat the oven to 200°C/400°F/Gas 6. If the parsnips are large and have woody centres, cut these out before cooking. The parsnips can be boiled in salted water for 2 minutes before roasting. This isn't essential, but if you prefer them 'overcooked' with a crispy skin and almost hollow but creamy centre, the par-boil will help.

2 Preheat a roasting tray on top of the stove and add the oil. Fry the parsnips in the oil until golden brown on all sides, allowing burnt tinges on the edges. Add the thyme leaves and roast in the oven, turning every 10 minutes, for 20–30 minutes, depending on size.

3 Remove from the oven and season with salt and pepper. Add the butter and honey. Return to the oven and cook for another 5–10 minutes. Place the parsnips in a serving dish and spoon over the juices to finish.

Spiced Apple Sauce

A CHANGE FROM THE NORMAL APPLE SAUCE, this goes very well with roast pork.

SERVES 6

500g (18oz) Bramley Seedling
    apples
25g (1oz) butter
2 tbsp water
2 tbsp white wine vinegar
¼ tsp freshly grated nutmeg
¼ tsp ground cinnamon
freshly ground black pepper
25g (1oz) soft dark brown sugar

1 Peel, core and cut up the apples.

2 Put them in a pan with the butter, water, vinegar and spices. Cover and cook gently until soft enough to beat to a purée. Add sugar to taste, and more spices if you like.

JAMES MARTIN'S EASY BRITISH FOOD

Roast Lamb

LAMB IS OFTEN SERVED WITH ROSEMARY SPRIGS AND GARLIC, but using lavender instead of rosemary contributes a subtly different flavour. And you might consider combining anchovies with meat – curious, but somehow the anchovies make the meat meatier!

SERVES 4

1 leg of lamb, about 2.25kg (5lb)
1 garlic bulb, cloves peeled
1 x 75g can anchovy fillets in
  olive oil
lots of tiny sprigs of fresh lavender
salt and freshly ground
  black pepper
about 2 tbsp lavender honey
  or lavender mustard
olive oil
2 lemons

FOR THE LAVENDER
HONEY GLAZE
100ml (3¹/₂fl oz) lavender honey
100ml (3¹/₂fl oz) olive oil

1 Preheat the oven to 180°C/350°F/Gas 4. Using a sharp knife, prick the leg of lamb all over, about 20 times and about 2cm (¾in) deep. Cut the garlic into thin strips and place one slice of garlic and a third of an anchovy fillet into each hole. Pick a sprig of lavender and place this into the holes, too. Continue until all the holes are full.

2 Place the joint in a roasting tray. Season with salt and pepper, and drizzle with lavender honey or spread with the lavender mustard. Roast in the oven for 1 hour 20 minutes for a 2.25kg (5lb) leg of lamb, basting every now and again.

3 Warm the honey for the glaze in a small pan, then, with a hand blender on a high speed, pour the oil in to create a warm glaze. Pour over the lamb, and return to the oven to cook for a further 20 minutes.

4 When the lamb is cooked, let it rest for 15 minutes before carving.

Real Mint Sauce

THIS WAS MY GRAN'S MINT SAUCE RECIPE. She never had a sharp knife, so she had to resort to chopping the mint in a grinder – this white plastic thing which you feed the leaves into while turning the handle. It did it in the end, but took about an hour to wash up …

SERVES 4

1 bunch fresh mint
pinch of salt
1 level tbsp caster sugar
4 tbsp boiling water
4 tbsp white wine vinegar

1 Strip the mint leaves off the stalks, sprinkle the leaves with the salt, and chop finely.

2 Place in a jug, add the sugar and pour over the boiling water. Stir and leave to cool.

3 Stir in the vinegar and taste. Add more water or vinegar, and adjust the seasoning to suit your taste.

Yorkshire Pudding

ONCE AGAIN, THIS IS MY GRAN'S RECIPE, which she used to serve with a rich onion gravy. I love these with foie gras pâté in the centre, served with the same gravy. This makes a great dinner party starter, and tastes fantastic.

SERVES 4

225g (8oz) plain flour
salt and freshly ground
*   black pepper*
8 medium free-range eggs
600ml (1 pint) milk
55g (2oz) good dripping or 50ml
*   (2fl oz) vegetable oil*

1 Place the flour and some seasoning in a bowl, and make a well in the middle. Add the eggs one by one, using a whisk, then whisk in the milk, mixing very well until the batter is smooth and there are no lumps. If possible, leave in the fridge for at least an hour or, even better, overnight.

2 Preheat the oven to about 220°C/425°F/Gas 7. Divide the dripping or vegetable oil between four Yorkshire pudding tins (about 13cm/5in in diameter) or muffin tins, and place in the oven to get very hot.

3 Carefully remove the trays from the oven and, with a ladle or from a jug, fill the tins with the batter and place back in the oven straight away. Cook for about 20 minutes before opening the door to check – otherwise they will collapse. If undercooked reduce the heat to 200°C/400°F/Gas 6, and cook for a further 10–15 minutes.

4 Remove from the oven and serve immediately.

Horseradish Sauce

THE BEST ACCOMPANIMENT to any roast beef or, indeed, steak.

MAKES 220ML (7FL OZ)

85g (3oz) fresh horseradish,
  peeled and finely grated
1 tsp Dijon or English mustard
1 tbsp white wine vinegar
1 tsp caster sugar
175ml (5fl oz) double cream,
  whipped
salt and freshly ground
  black pepper

1 Place all the ingredients except the seasoning in a bowl, and whisk together to a soft peak consistency. Season with salt and pepper.

2 The sauce is best served chilled.

Roast Potatoes

EVERYONE LOVES ROAST POTATOES, and they go with any roast.

SERVES 6

10 medium King Edward,
  Maris Piper or Desirée potatoes
good pinch of salt
50g (1¾oz) lard or dripping
  (use vegetable oil if you don't
  have either)

1 Preheat the oven to 200°C/400°F/Gas 6. Peel the potatoes and cut each one in half (into three if the potatoes are large). Place in a saucepan, cover with cold water and add the salt. Bring to the boil and simmer for a maximum of 3–4 minutes. Pour into a colander and allow to drain well.

2 Heat the lard or dripping in a roasting tray on the stove, and fry the potatoes until they start to brown. Turn them occasionally. Sprinkle generously with salt, then roast for about 30 minutes, before removing and turning them in the tray in order to prevent them from sticking. Roast for another 30 minutes and remove. Serve immediately.

Peppered Roast Beef

WHAT CAN I SAY ABOUT ROAST BEEF THAT HASN'T BEEN SAID ALREADY? Anyway, the picture says it all. I was brought up on this every week, and it's one of the best things we produce in the UK. When I was about 14, I went to work in two two-star Michelin restaurants in France and got treated like a skivvy for 10 weeks, as both head chefs thought all we did was roast beef and Yorkshire pudding. Roast beef – they don't know what they're missing.

SERVES 8

675–900g (1½–2lb)
  topside, sirloin or rib of beef
2–3 tbsp black peppercorns,
  finely crushed
salt
cooking fat or oil
large sprig of rosemary

1 Preheat the oven to 220°C/425°F/Gas 7. Roll the beef in the crushed peppercorns until completely covered. Season with salt.

2 Heat some oil in a hot roasting pan, then add the meat to seal. Remove from the heat and tuck a sprig of rosemary underneath the meat or place it on top. Roast in the oven – a joint of this size will take between 25 and 40 minutes to cook, but this very much depends on how you would like to eat it. Cooking for 20 minutes will keep it rare; 30 minutes, medium; and 40 minutes, medium-to-well-done.

3 Once cooked, leave the meat to rest for 15–20 minutes before carving. This will relax the meat, and it will become even more tender.

Easy Gravy

THIS GOES BEST WITH ROASTS, but it's also great with sausages and mash, or with Yorkshire pudding.

SERVES 4–6

100ml (3½fl oz) vegetable
  cooking water
3 white onions, peeled and
  thinly sliced
25g (1oz) butter
4 tbsp Bisto powder
150ml (5fl oz) red wine
¾ tsp mustard powder
1 tsp cornflour

1 Remove the roasted meat from the roasting tray, and pour off any excess fat. Add the vegetable water to the remaining juices in the tray, and slowly simmer over a low heat on the stove top, stirring to remove any bits from the bottom of the tray.

2 Meanwhile, in a separate pan, fry the onions in the butter to give them a brown colour.

3 Dissolve the Bisto in 600ml (1 pint) hot water. Pour this into the roasting tray with the red wine, and add the onion.

4 In a small dish, stir the mustard powder and cornflour into a little water to make a paste. Whisk into the gravy, and cook for about 10 minutes more, until thickened and full of flavour.

Roast Chicken

ROAST CHICKEN IS EVERYONE'S FAVOURITE, and this is a simple recipe given an extra little kick of flavour by the lemon.

SERVES 4

*1 free-range chicken, cleaned
  and trussed, about 1.3kg (3lb)*
olive oil
*salt and freshly ground
  black pepper*
knob of butter
6 slices streaky bacon
2 fresh lemons

1 Preheat the oven to 200°C/400°F/Gas 6. Brush the bird all over with olive oil and season generously. Put the knob of butter inside the bird, and place the bacon over the breast part of the chicken. Place in an oven tray.

2 Cut the lemons in half and place around the chicken, then drizzle everything with a little more olive oil.

3 Roast in the oven for 20 minutes per 450g (1lb), basting frequently. Push a skewer into the thigh at the thickest point. If the juices run clear, it is done; if not, give it another 5 minutes.

4 Leave the cooked bird to stand in a warm place for 15 minutes before carving. This standing time is vital. The bird finishes cooking while the juices are recovered and absorbed back into the meat, making every slice moist.

Duck with Orange

I LOVE 1970S FOOD – the Berni Inn, the prawn cocktail, the chicken in a basket and duck à l'orange. It's fine to embrace the future, but don't ever forget the past. I did this the other day for a dinner party, and it went down a storm. I gave them prawn cocktail to start and a Black Forest gâteau for pudding. Serve with some extra orange slices, briefly caramelised in butter, if you like.

SERVES 2

4 tsp runny honey
40g (1½oz) butter
2 x 200g (7oz) duck breasts
salt and freshly ground
*   black pepper*

FOR THE SAUCE
40g (1½oz) butter
1 rounded tbsp plain flour
500ml (18fl oz) hot duck,
*   game or beef stock*
2 Seville oranges, or 2 sweet
*   oranges and 1 lemon*
1 tbsp caster sugar
4 tbsp Port

1 Make the sauce first. Melt the butter in a small pan and let it turn a delicate golden brown colour. Stir in the flour, cook for 2 minutes, then add the stock. Allow to simmer gently for at least 20 minutes – the longer the better. Meanwhile, preheat the oven to 200°C/400°F/Gas 6.

2 To cook the duck, melt the honey and butter together in a very hot pan, then place the duck in, skin-side down. Season well with salt and pepper, and colour very well (until almost black) before turning over. Place on an oven tray and bake for 8–10 minutes, until pink. Once cooked, remove from the oven and allow to rest. Reserve any juices from the pan for use in the sauce.

3 Meanwhile, remove the peel thinly from the oranges, and cut it into matchstick strips. Simmer these in boiling water for 3 minutes, then drain and add to the simmering sauce. Add the juice of the oranges, and lemon to the sauce, if used. Stir in some sugar to taste; start with a little, and add more if necessary. Finally, pour in the reserved meat juices from the duck, which should be well skimmed of fat, then the Port.

4 To serve, slice the duck breast, pour the sauce over it, and serve.

PUDDINGS

Ice-creams at Whitby

Raspberry Pavlova

NAMED AFTER A BALLERINA, THIS IS A NATIONAL DISH IN AUSTRALIA, but we love it here as our own. I have made the pavlova in a slightly different way, in what is called boiled or Italian meringue; I think this is the best way to make a pavlova. My top tip with a pavlova is to fill it full of fruit in season.

SERVES 4

280g (10oz) caster sugar
5 free-range egg whites

TO SERVE
100g (3½oz) white chocolate,
   melted
250ml (9fl oz) double cream,
   whipped
5 punnets fresh raspberries
icing sugar, for dusting
a few sprigs of mint

1 Preheat the oven to 120°C/250°F/Gas ½, and cover a large tray with nonstick baking parchment. In a pan, boil 100ml (3½fl oz) water and the sugar to the soft ball stage (115°C/239°F). Remove from the heat.

2 Whisk up the egg whites in a bowl, and pour in the liquid sugar while still beating. Keep on beating until the mixture is cool. Spoon the mixture on to the tray, and spread it out into four circles. Using a spoon, mould the centres into a pavlova shape, with an indentation. Place the tray in the oven and cook for 3–4 hours, or overnight.

3 Remove from the oven, cool, then arrange on a plate. Spread the melted white chocolate across the top of each meringue (this will stop the cream softening it). Leave to set.

4 Fill the indentation with double cream, top with raspberries, a little dusting of icing sugar and a sprig of mint, and serve.

Strawberry Terrine with a Cinnamon Sugar Doughnut

THIS IS BASED ON A SEMIFREDDO. You can use most soft fruits that are in season, and nougat or meringue added to the mixture is also really nice. A simple, great-tasting dessert that you can make, keep in the freezer and take a slice of whenever you fancy.

SERVES 4–6

4 free-range eggs, separated
4 tbsp caster sugar
1 vanilla pod, split
400g (14oz) mascarpone cheese
200g (7oz) fresh strawberries,
    diced
olive oil

FOR THE STRAWBERRY SAUCE
300g (10½oz) fresh strawberries,
    diced
50ml (2fl oz) water
2 tbsp icing sugar

FOR THE STRAWBERRY COMPOTE
115g (4oz) fresh strawberries,
    diced
50ml (2fl oz) strawberry sauce
    (see above)
4 leaves fresh mint, finely chopped

FOR THE GARNISH
2 tbsp caster sugar
1 tsp ground cinnamon
4 small doughnuts (the
    supermarket mini ones are OK)
4 sprigs fresh mint

1 Put the egg yolks in one bowl, and the whites in another. Add the sugar to the egg yolks, along with the seeds from the vanilla pod, and whisk until very light and frothy. Add the mascarpone and keep mixing.

2 Whip up the egg whites to stiff peaks, then fold them into the mascarpone mixture carefully, along with the strawberries.

3 Grease a 450g (1lb) loaf tin with olive oil, then line with clingfilm. Pour the mixture into the mould, and freeze until set, overnight if possible.

4 For the strawberry sauce, blend all the ingredients together, then pass through a sieve. For the strawberry compote, simply mix all the ingredients together.

5 Mix the caster sugar and cinnamon powder together in a bowl, and add the doughnuts one at a time to coat them.

6 Tip the iced terrine from the tin and slice. Place a slice on each plate, with a doughnut alongside. Put a little strawberry compote in the doughnut hole, garnish with a sprig of fresh mint and pour around some of the remaining strawberry sauce.

Rhubarb and Elderflower Jelly

YORKSHIRE IS FAB FOR A LOT OF FOODIE THINGS, BUT IN THE AREA OF BRADFORD, Leeds and Wakefield the most famous ingredient is rhubarb. These three cities form the area of the rhubarb triangle, which is where the best rhubarb in England and indeed the world comes from. It's grown in two main forms, outside and inside, the outside being the thicker-stemmed type requiring sugar to sweeten it. The inside variety is produced in the darkness in pitch black sheds and is known as 'forced'. For this the roots are grown outside, then carefully removed from the ground, washed and placed in the sheds on the floor. They are then given only water and warmth, and the stems start to grow in complete darkness, becoming pale and sweet. The season is once a year, and the stems are harvested by candlelight and picked one by one by hand. If you're ever up in that area in March or the beginning of April, go to see this stuff growing, it really is something special.

SERVES 4

500g (18oz) forced rhubarb
4 tbsp caster sugar
3 free-range egg whites
250ml (9fl oz) double cream
juice and finely grated zest
    of 2 oranges

TO SERVE
55g (2oz) toasted cracked oatmeal
4 strawberries
4 sprigs fresh mint

1 Preheat the oven to 200°C/400°F/Gas 6. First, wash and cut the stems of rhubarb into 5cm (2in) pieces. Place in an ovenproof dish and sprinkle with the sugar and 4 tbsp water. Bake for about 20 minutes, until soft. Remove from the oven and allow to cool.

2 Meanwhile, whip up the egg whites and cream – separately – to soft peaks. Fold the rhubarb into the cream, together with the orange juice and zest, then fold in the whipped egg whites.

3 Spoon the mixture into four glasses and chill, before serving each one topped with the toasted oatmeal, a strawberry and a sprig of mint.

Gooseberry Fool

IN MY GARDEN THESE ARE ONE OF THE FIRST FRUITS OF THE SPRING, but we in this country seem to be the only people to embrace this fantastic fruit. Other than with mackerel, I feel the gooseberry should just be used for puddings and puddings alone. It is good in a pie and in a fool, or it can be simply served with vanilla ice-cream.

SERVES 6–8

55g (2oz) butter
500g (18oz) young green
  gooseberries, topped and tailed
caster sugar
300ml (10fl oz) double cream,
  or half each single and
  double cream
juice and finely grated zest
  of 1 orange

1 Melt the butter in a large pan, add the gooseberries, cover and leave to cook gently for about 5 minutes. When the fruit looks yellow and softened, remove the pan from the heat and crush the fruit with a wooden spoon, then a fork. Do not try to produce too smooth a purée by sieving or liquidising the gooseberries; they should be more of a mash. Sweeten with sugar to taste. Allow to cool.

2 Whip the cream(s) until you have half-whipped but soft peaks, and fold in the cooled fruit, orange juice and most of the zest. Taste and add more sugar if necessary, but do not make the fool too sweet.

3 Serve lightly chilled, sprinkled with the remaining orange zest, and accompanied by almond biscuits or shortbread.

Treacle Tart

SYRUP AND BREAD IN PASTRY ... whoever invented this? But whoever you are, what a combination! I feel, though, that you must eat this warm and never place it in the fridge. Serve with double cream, ice-cream, whipped cream or with fruit. I'll leave it up to you.

SERVES 10

butter, for greasing
500g (18oz) ready-made
  sweet pastry
plain flour, for rolling
about 400g (14oz) golden syrup
125g (4^1/$_2$oz) fresh breadcrumbs
2 free-range eggs, lightly beaten
finely grated zest and juice
  of 1 lemon
whipped cream, to serve

1 Preheat the oven to 180°C/350°F/Gas 4, and butter a 35cm (14in) ovenproof tart tin.

2 Roll out the pastry on a floured surface until very thin and, using the tart tin as a template, cut around the dish, allowing enough to go up the sides of the tin. Place the disc of pastry in the bottom of the dish and up over the sides. Prick the base with a fork, and bake for 10–12 minutes, until lightly golden. Remove from the oven, and lower the oven temperature to 140°C/275°F/Gas 1.

3 In a bowl, mix together the golden syrup, breadcrumbs, eggs and lemon juice and zest. Once combined, spoon into the pastry case and bake at the reduced temperature for 50–60 minutes.

4 Trim off the edges of the pastry, and cut the tart into portions. Allow the tart to cool slightly before serving. It is best eaten warm, with a spoonful of whipped cream.

Bakewell Tart

BAKEWELL TART AND BAKEWELL PUDDING ARE MORE OR LESS THE SAME, but the original did not contain almonds, and was more like a custard tart. One tip for this is to mix the ingredients well at the start, as this will make the mixture lighter and give a nicer texture.

SERVES 10

115g (4oz) caster sugar
55g (2oz) ground almonds
125g (4½oz) plain flour, plus extra
   for dusting
100g (3½oz) butter, finely diced
1 large free-range egg, plus 1 extra
   yolk
finely grated zest of 1 small lemon
pinch of salt

FOR THE FILLING
85g (3oz) butter
85g (3oz) caster sugar
2 medium free-range eggs
3 drops almond essence
55g (2oz) fresh white breadcrumbs
85g (3oz) ground almonds
8 tbsp raspberry jam
20g (¾oz) flaked almonds

1 First, make the pastry. Put the sugar, almonds and flour into a food processor, and turn on to full speed for a few seconds. Add the diced butter and work again until just blended in. The mixture will resemble fine breadcrumbs.

2 Add the egg and extra yolk, the lemon zest, 2 tsp water and a tiny pinch of salt. Work again until the pastry balls. Wrap in clingfilm and refrigerate. Preheat the oven to 190°C/375°F/Gas 5.

3 Roll out the chilled pastry on a flour-dusted surface and use to line a 20cm (8in) loose-bottomed tart tin. If it breaks it can be repaired by pressing with your fingers. Make the shell as even as possible, and ensure that around the edges it is pushed right up to the top, as it will shrink as it bakes. Be careful to press into the bottom edges to eliminate air between the tin and pastry.

4 To make the filling, put the butter and sugar in a blender, and blend until light and fluffy. With the machine running on full speed, add the eggs and almond essence until combined to a smooth paste, then fold in the breadcrumbs and ground almonds.

5 Put the pastry shell on a baking tray, prick the base with a fork and line with foil. Fill with baking beans and bake blind for 10 minutes. Remove the foil and beans, and leave to cool slightly, then fill the base with a layer of raspberry jam. Cover this with the almond filling. Scrape the surface smooth and level, and sprinkle with the flaked almonds.

6 Return to the oven and bake for 25–30 minutes, until risen and lightly browned.

Puff Pastry Hearts with Cream and Jam

SUCH A SIMPLE IDEA, THIS, USING READY-MADE PUFF PASTRY, but don't refrigerate the pastry once cooked as it will become too hard. Glazing it in this way with icing sugar requires a very hot oven.

MAKES 15–20

300g (10½oz) ready-rolled
  puff pastry
plain flour, for dusting
8 tbsp caster sugar
1 tbsp ground cinnamon
150ml (5fl oz) double cream
85g (3oz) raspberry
  or strawberry jam

1 If necessary, roll out the pastry on a floured work surface until it is about 5mm (¼in) thick. You should have a rectangle of about 30 x 20cm (12 x 8in).

2 Mix the caster sugar and cinnamon together in a bowl. Brush the pastry with some water, then sprinkle some of the spiced sugar liberally over the top. Fold each long side over to meet in the middle.

3 Brush the top with water again, then sprinkle again with some of the sugar, then repeat the above, folding the long sides over to meet in the middle. Brush with water and sprinkle with the sugar again, and fold over. You should have eight layers. Place in the fridge to chill.

4 Meanwhile, preheat the oven to 200°C/400°F/Gas 6. Using a sharp knife, cut the pastry into strips about 5mm (¼in) wide and place on an oven tray with the cut side up. Bake for 10–15 minutes to open to a heart shape and take on a golden brown colour. Remove from the oven and allow to cool completely.

5 While cooling, whip up the double cream until stiff, and place in a piping bag with a plain or starred nozzle. Take one of the heart-shaped pastries and add a spoon of the jam in the middle. Pipe the double cream on top. Add another piece of pastry on top – at a slant so you can see the filling inside – and serve.

Jam or Marmalade Roly Poly

YOU MAY HAVE BEEN PUT OFF THESE TYPES OF HOMELY DESSERTS BY THOSE SERVED AT SCHOOL. But try this one or, better still, serve it at a smart dinner party, and everyone will love it. Let's face it, what could be better …

SERVES 4–6

225g (8oz) self-raising flour
1 tsp baking powder
pinch of salt
finely grated zest of 1 lemon
 or orange
140g (5oz) vegetarian or beef suet
100–150ml (3½–5fl oz) milk, plus
 extra for brushing
140–175g (5–6oz) orange
 marmalade or raspberry jam

1 Sift together the flour, baking powder and salt into a bowl. Add the lemon or orange zest, and suet, and rub the mixture gently with your fingertips until it resembles breadcrumbs. Add the milk a little at a time, and squeeze with your hands until a soft texture is formed. Wrap in clingfilm and allow to rest in the fridge for 20–30 minutes.

2 Roll the dough into a rectangle approximately 35 x 25cm (14 x 10in). Spread the marmalade or jam on the dough, leaving a border of 1cm (½in) clear. Brush the border with extra milk or water.

3 Roll the dough from the shorter edge and pinch at either end to retain all of the marmalade or jam. Wrap the roly poly loosely in greaseproof paper, followed by loose foil, and tie with string at either end.

4 Steam the pudding in a steamer for 2 hours, topping up with hot water, if necessary, during cooking. Once cooked, unwrap, slice and serve (it's great with custard or ice-cream).

Apple Fritters with Vanilla Ice-cream

CHINESE RESTAURANTS DO GREAT FRITTERS – a simple light batter coated over the fruit and deep-fried with toffee and sometimes some sesame seeds. Whichever way you do fritters, they are always a winner.

SERVES 6

6 large Cox's Orange Pippins,
    or other firm eating apples
caster sugar, to taste
good dash of brandy
vegetable oil for deep-frying
vanilla ice-cream, to serve

FOR THE BATTER
115g (4oz) plain flour
1 free-range egg plus 1 yolk
1 tbsp oil or clarified butter
up to 300ml (10fl oz) milk
pinch of saffron strands (optional)

1 Peel, core and slice the apples thickly. Put them into a dish, sprinkle with sugar and pour on the brandy. Leave them to one side for an hour or so, turning occasionally in the liquid. Drain well before coating them with batter.

2 Meanwhile, for the batter, mix the flour, egg, egg yolk and oil or clarified butter. Beat in about half the milk. Pour 3 tbsp of almost boiling water over the saffron, if using, and leave to steep for a little while. When the water is a good crocus yellow, strain it into the batter. Add more milk if the batter is too thick.

3 Heat the vegetable oil in a deep-fryer to 180°C/350°F. Dip the apple slices into the batter, and fry them in hot oil until golden brown. Serve sprinkled with sugar, with a scoop of vanilla ice-cream.

Poached Pears with Cinnamon and Goat's Milk Sauce

IF YOU LOOK AT THIS RECIPE, YOU'LL WONDER HOW THE HELL THE SAUCE WORKS. Well, I can't tell you how; it just does. One thing, though, within reason the more you cook the sauce, the better it is (it should be a dark caramel colour). Oh, and one more thing: cook it in a large pan because when you add the baking powder it will boil all over the place.

SERVES 4

1 vanilla pod, split in half
*   lengthways*
200g (7oz) caster sugar
4 Comice pears
juice and finely grated zest
*   of 1 lemon*
1 x 200g tub good vanilla
*   ice-cream*

FOR THE SAUCE
600ml (1 pint) goat's milk
200g (7oz) caster sugar
50ml (2fl oz) golden syrup
1 cinnamon stick
1 tsp baking powder

1 Start the sauce by putting the milk, sugar and golden syrup in a pan. Bring to the boil. Crumble the cinnamon stick into the milk and add the baking powder. Take the pan off the heat and stir well as the mix will rise quickly. Continue to whisk the mixture until it stops rising.

2 Place the sauce on the heat again and bring back to the boil, whisking all the time. Turn down the heat and simmer for about 45 minutes, stirring from time to time to prevent the mixture from burning. When the sauce is ready it should be a caramel colour. Burnt or black is no good.

3 Meanwhile, place the vanilla pod in a pan with the sugar. Peel the pears, leaving the stalks on, and use the peeler to remove the core from the bottom of the pears. Place in the pan with the sugar and vanilla, and cover with hot water. Pour in the lemon juice and zest, and cover. Bring to the boil with the lid on. Turn down the heat and simmer for 20–30 minutes, until the pears are cooked, testing them with a knife.

4 Remove the pears from the pan and drain for a minute on kitchen paper. Using a sharp knife, fan the pears by cutting five slits in each of them. Place the pears on serving plates, pour the hot sauce over the top and serve with vanilla ice-cream.

Chocolate Profiteroles

CHOCOLATE ECLAIRS AND PROFITEROLES WERE MY DOWNFALL, causing me to get to nearly 20 stone while I was working as a pastry chef in a hotel. I used to eat about 20 of them before 11 in the morning. What a pig I was, but, even worse, I would be eating about 20 pains au chocolat as well .... They tasted good, though ...

MAKES 28

200ml (7fl oz) cold water
4 tsp caster sugar
85g (3oz) unsalted butter
115g (4oz) plain flour
pinch of salt
4 medium free-range eggs, beaten
vegetable oil, for greasing

FOR THE CREAM FILLING
600ml (1 pint) double cream

FOR THE CHOCOLATE SAUCE
175g (6oz) good-quality plain
   chocolate, broken into pieces
5 tbsp water
15g (½oz) butter

1 Preheat the oven to 200°C/400°F/Gas 6. To make the pastry, place the water, sugar and butter in a large saucepan. Place over a low heat to melt the butter. Increase the heat and shoot in the flour and salt all in one go. Remove from the heat and quickly beat the mixture vigorously with a wooden spoon until a smooth paste is formed, stirring continuously to dry out the paste. Once the paste curls away from the side of the pan, transfer the mixture to a large bowl and leave to cool for 10–15 minutes.

2 Beat in the eggs, a little at a time, until the paste is smooth and glossy. Continue adding the eggs until you have a soft dropping consistency. It may not be necessary to add all the eggs. The mixture will be shiny and smooth, and will fall from a spoon if it is given a sharp jerk.

3 Lightly oil a large baking tray. Dip a teaspoon into some warm water and spoon out 1 tsp of the profiterole mixture. Rub the top of the mixture with a wet finger and spoon on to the baking tray. This ensures a crisper topping. Cover the whole of the tray with dollops of pastry, working as swiftly as you can. Place the tray in the oven and, before closing the door, throw a little water into the bottom of the oven. Shut the door quickly. This will make more steam in the oven and make the choux pastry rise better. Top pastry chef tip there!

4 Bake for 25–30 minutes, until golden brown. Remove from the oven and prick the base of each profiterole. Place on to the baking tray with the hole facing upwards and return to the oven for 5 minutes. The warm air from the oven helps to dry the middle of the profiteroles.

5 To prepare the filling, lightly whip the cream until soft peaks form. Do not overwhip. When the profiteroles are cold, use a piping bag with a plain nozzle to pipe the cream into the holes of the profiteroles.

6 To make the sauce, melt the chocolate with the water and butter in a bowl over a pan of boiling water. Stir without boiling until smooth and shiny. Arrange the buns on a dish and pour over the hot sauce. Eat hot or cold.

Baked Chocolate Mousse

THIS MOUSSE-CAKE CONTAINS NO FLOUR AND NEEDS TO BE BAKED AND EATEN FRESH. As it starts to cool it will collapse, but don't worry – it still eats well, so long as you don't put it in the fridge.

SERVES 6–8

300g (10½oz) dark bitter
   chocolate, broken into pieces
140g (5oz) unsalted butter, diced
6 free-range eggs, separated
55g (2oz) caster sugar
double cream, to serve

1 Line the base and sides of a 20cm (8in) spring-bottomed cake tin with greaseproof paper, and preheat the oven to 180°C/350°F/Gas 4.

2 Melt the chocolate and butter in a metal bowl over a pan of simmering water. Whisk the egg yolks with 2 tbsp of the sugar. Stir in the melted chocolate and mix well.

3 Beat the egg whites with the remaining sugar until very stiff. Quickly fold one-third of the whites into the chocolate mix, then gently fold in the remainder and pour the mix into the prepared cake tin. Place on the middle shelf of the oven and bake for 20 minutes.

4 Remove from the oven and leave to cool slightly, before serving with the double cream poured over.

Lemon Verbena Crème Brûlée

I GROW LEMON VERBENA IN MY GARDEN – it is so nice, even the dog likes eating it. You have to get some of this herb for your garden at home, as its smell and flavour are different to any other herb. I use it mainly for desserts, as the flavour lends itself well to being infused in a liquid, as in this crème brûlée.

**SERVES 4–6,
DEPENDING ON SIZE
OF RAMEKINS**

250ml (9fl oz) milk
*5 sprigs fresh lemon verbena,
  chopped*
10 free-range egg yolks
175g (6oz) caster sugar
750ml (26fl oz) double cream
55g (2oz) demerara sugar

1 Preheat the oven to 120°C/250°F/Gas ½. Heat the milk in a pan with the lemon verbena until just boiling, then remove from the heat to cool and allow the flavours to blend.

2 Place the egg yolks in a bowl, add the caster sugar and whisk together until combined. Add the milk and cream, and whisk well. Pass through a sieve to remove any egg shell and the lemon verbena.

3 Ladle the mixture into small ramekins, and place in the oven for 1½–2 hours, until set. Remove and allow to cool. Either refrigerate or use straight away.

4 When ready to eat them, sprinkle the demerara sugar over the top and caramelise with either a blow torch or by putting under a hot grill.

Orange Marmalade Ice-cream

I MADE THIS WHILE PLAYING WITH MY NEW ICE-CREAM MACHINE, and it works, but be careful of the sugar in the recipe. Standard recipes for ice-cream say 225g (8oz) of sugar per litre (1$^3/_4$ pints) of liquid, but sugar will act as a de-icer, and the ice-cream won't freeze properly if there is too much. The same applies to alcohol, so remember to reduce the quantity if making a high-sugar or alcoholic ice-cream. This ice-cream is great served with seasonal fresh berries, or fab with a toasted croissant and some hot chocolate sauce.

MAKES 1.2 LITRES (2 PINTS)

1 vanilla pod
250ml (9fl oz) milk
750ml (26fl oz) double cream
175g (6oz) caster sugar
10 free-range egg yolks
6 tbsp orange marmalade

1 Taking a sharp knife, cut the vanilla pod in half lengthways, and scrape out and retain the seeds.

2 Place the milk, cream, vanilla seeds and pod, and caster sugar in a pan, and bring to the boil.

3 In a separate bowl whisk the egg yolks. When the cream mixture has boiled, pour the mixture slowly on to the eggs, whisking all the time. Pour into a clean pan and mix quickly over a gentle heat until the mixture has thickened. Pass through a sieve.

4 Place the mixture into an ice-cream machine and churn until the ice-cream is nearly set. Add the marmalade and continue to churn. Once set, transfer the ice-cream from the machine into a container, and place in the freezer.

Instant Banana Ice-cream

THIS MAY BE INSTANT, but it is one of the most delicious ice-creams.

SERVES 4-6

4 bananas
¼ tsp vanilla essence
3–4 tbsp caster sugar, to taste
150ml (5fl oz) buttermilk

1 Peel the bananas, cut into chunks and place in a single layer on a freezer-proof dish or tray, as you would raspberries, then freeze so that you have separate pieces.

2 Tip the frozen banana chunks into the food processor. Add the vanilla, sugar and half the buttermilk.

3 Turn on the processor and let it run for a few moments. Then, while it is still running, pour in the remaining buttermilk in a thin, steady stream. Let the machine run until the mixture is smooth and creamy. Serve at once.

Apricot Yoghurt Ice-cream

THIS IS SUCH A GREAT IDEA. It's so quick and easy, and works with most puréed fruit. Strawberries work best after apricots, I think, as the orange juice complements their taste.

SERVES 20

650g (1lb 7oz) apricot purée
350g (12oz) icing sugar
2 vanilla pods
1 tbsp Amaretto
50ml (2fl oz) liquid glucose
90ml (3fl oz) orange juice
300g (10½oz) Greek yoghurt
250ml (9fl oz) crème fraîche

1 Slowly stir the apricot purée into the icing sugar to form a paste.

2 Using a sharp knife, split the vanilla pods lengthways, and scrape the seeds out into the apricot purée. Mix in the remaining ingredients, and whisk until smooth.

3 Churn in an ice-cream machine until it is just set, then place in a container in the freezer. Allow to defrost a little before serving

TEAS AND CAKES

Betty's Café Tea Rooms in York

Cheese Straws

I LIKE THESE WITH ANCHOVIES INSIDE, but you can leave them out if you want. If you are going to add them, buy those preserved in olive oil – these have less salt in them, and will taste much better inside the straw.

MAKES 24

1 x 375g packet ready-rolled
  puff pastry
55g (2oz) unsalted butter, melted
10 anchovies, drained and
  blended to a paste
2 tbsp sun-dried tomato paste
55g (2oz) Parmesan, freshly grated
2 tbsp chopped fresh flat-leaf
  parsley
sea salt
1 free-range egg yolk, beaten with
  1 tbsp water

1 Preheat the oven to 220°C/425°F/Gas 7. Place the pastry on a floured work surface, roll out slightly, then cut to create two squares. Using a large, sharp knife, trim the edges of the pastry so that the straws cook uniformly. Brush the pastry lightly with the melted butter.

2 Spread the first pastry half with the anchovies. Spread the other piece of pastry with the sun-dried tomato paste. Sprinkle both with Parmesan, parsley and some salt. Fold the bottom half of each piece over the top half, and gently press down. Roll out a bit to compress the filling. Brush the pastry with the beaten egg.

3 With a large, sharp knife, cut the pastry, lengthways, into 1cm (½in) strips. Hold the ends between your fingers and carefully stretch and twist the strips in opposite directions.

4 Place the twisted strips on to lightly oiled baking sheets, spacing them evenly apart. Bake for 10–12 minutes, or until crisp and golden.

5 Remove the cheese straws from the oven and allow to cool on the baking sheet for 5 minutes to firm up. Using a palette knife, carefully transfer the cheese straws to a wire rack or serving plate.

Griddle Scones

THESE ARE SO GOOD EATEN WARM WITH SOME BUTTER OR WITH JAM. But if you leave them to go cold they can be eaten like normal scones with jam and whipped cream.

MAKES 20

225g (8oz) plain flour
1¹/₂ tsp baking powder
15g (¹/₂oz) caster sugar
pinch of salt
1 free-range egg, beaten
about 150ml (5fl oz) full-fat milk
knob of butter, for frying

1 Sieve the flour into a bowl with the baking powder, sugar and salt. Make a well in the middle, put in the egg, then the milk, and whisk to a thick batter, adding a little more milk if the mixture is too dry (you want the consistency of double cream). Leave to stand for 30 minutes at room temperature before using.

2 Preheat the frying pan, add a little butter, and test by cooking one scone first, then cook the rest in batches. 1 tbsp of batter will make one scone. As the bottom of the scones cook, after about 2 minutes, bubbles will come to the surface. Turn them on to the other side and cook for a further 2 minutes.

3 Keep the scones warm, wrapped in a cloth in a low oven, until all are done. Eat while still warm, with butter and jam.

Gingerbread Biscuits

GINGERBREAD MEN NEVER USED TO REACH THE BISCUIT TIN at my Gran's house when I was there. This recipe is more than 40 years old, and tastes the same every time I make it. But bear in mind if you have ground spices such as ginger in your cupboard, eight times out of ten, you will have bought them for a dish some years before. Once the label has changed colour and the best-before date says something like 1972, the spices are knackered and you should buy fresh.

MAKES ABOUT 20

225g (8oz) plain flour

1/4 tsp salt

2 tsp bicarbonate of soda

1 heaped tsp ground ginger

1/4 tsp ground cinnamon

55g (2oz) unsalted butter

115g (4oz) soft brown sugar

115g (4oz) golden syrup

1 tbsp evaporated milk

1 Sift the flour, salt, bicarbonate of soda and spices together into a bowl. Heat the butter, sugar and syrup together until dissolved, then leave to cool. Once cooled, mix into the dry ingredients with the evaporated milk to make a dough. Chill for 30 minutes.

2 Preheat the oven to 190°C/375°F/Gas 5 and grease two baking sheets. Roll out the biscuit dough to about 5mm (¼in) thick and cut into fingers, circles or even gingerbread men.

3 Place on the baking sheets, allowing a little space to spread, and bake for 10–15 minutes. Remove from the oven. Leave to cool slightly on the baking sheets before transferring to a wire rack.

NB An additional 1 tsp of finely chopped fresh ginger can be added for a stronger ginger flavour.

Doughnuts

WORTH THE WAIT, trust me.

MAKES 5–10

250g (9oz) strong white flour,
plus extra for dusting
pinch of salt
40g (1½oz) caster sugar,
plus extra to coat
25g (1oz) butter, softened
150ml (5fl oz) water
20g (¾oz) easy-blend yeast
some good jam (optional)
vegetable or sunflower oil, for
deep-frying

1 Put all the ingredients except the jam, oil and coating sugar into a large bowl and mix together. Tip out on to a lightly floured surface and knead for 5 minutes. Put the dough back in the bowl, cover with a cloth, and leave for about 1 hour, until doubled in size.

2 Divide the dough into 85g (3oz) pieces and shape into balls. If you want, put 1 tsp jam inside each ball. Put on your floured surface and leave to rise until doubled in size again.

3 Pour some oil into a large heavy-based pan and heat to 170ºC/340ºF, or a medium heat. Lower each of the doughnuts into the oil and fry until brown, then roll them over and fry the other side. (If you have a problem with rolling the doughnuts over, then pierce them slightly with a knife to help you.) The frying should take no more than 5 minutes for both sides.

4 When they are browned, drain on kitchen paper and tip them straight into a bowl full of caster sugar and coat well. Cool on a wire rack, then enjoy with a nice cup of tea.

Yorkshire Brack

ELIZABETH BOTHAM, A COFFEE AND CAKE SHOP IN WHITBY, was where I first tasted Yorkshire brack. It's a bit like a fruit cake, but lighter, and has the taste and texture of sticky toffee pudding. They have either tea-infused or ginger-flavoured brack, and it's made fresh on the premises. When in there, try the lemon buns, which is what they're famous for – they taste great. While walking round the town afterwards with a bag of brack in one hand, and a sticky lemon bun in the other, do the local thing: split the bun in half and turn the top over to make it look like a sandwich – you won't look so much like a tourist! Sorry, almost forgot, buy two buns while you're at it, as it's a long walk back up the hill for another one …

SERVES 6–8

675g (1¹/₂lb) golden raisins
675g (1¹/₂lb) dark raisins
450g (1lb) light brown sugar
250ml (9fl oz) cold strong
   breakfast tea
125ml (4fl oz) whisky or bourbon
550g (1¹/₄lb) plain flour
4 tsp baking powder
large pinch of salt
1 tsp freshly grated nutmeg
1 tsp ground allspice
3 free-range eggs, beaten
finely grated rind of 1 lemon

1 Soak the raisins and sugar in the tea and whisky in a large bowl for 12 hours or overnight.

2 The next day, preheat the oven to 150–160°C/300–325°F/Gas 2–3, and grease a 25cm (10in) round cake tin.

3 Sift together the flour, baking powder, salt, nutmeg and allspice, and add to the raisin mixture along with the beaten eggs and lemon rind. Combine well.

4 Put the batter in the greased tin, and bake for 60–80 minutes until firm to the touch.

5 When done, remove from the pan and let it cool on a wire rack. You can leave it simple and serve it with butter, or top it with a little icing.

Shortbread Sugar Thins

THERE ARE MANY VARIATIONS OF SHORTBREAD, and in this book I have given you three of them. This one is more like a biscuit.

MAKES AS MANY AS YOU LIKE

250g (9oz) butter
250g (9oz) caster sugar,
  plus extra to sprinkle
1 free-range egg, beaten
1 tbsp double cream
300g (10½oz) plain flour
½ tsp salt
1 tsp baking powder
few drops of vanilla essence (or
  lemon juice or 2 tsp ground
  ginger)

1 Cream the butter and sugar together, then add all the remaining ingredients. Mix well. If you like, you can divide the dough into three, and flavour each part differently (with vanilla, lemon juice and ground ginger).

2 Form the dough into a long roll or rolls, about 5cm (2in) in diameter, and wrap in foil. Put in the fridge until the next day.

3 Preheat the oven to 190ºC/375ºF/Gas 5. Shave off the dough into the thinnest possible slices. Put them on a baking tray, sprinkle them with sugar and cook them for 5 minutes only. They should remain pale in colour.

4 There is no need to bake the dough all at once; cut off what you need and put the excess back in the fridge or the freezer.

Grandma's Caramel Banana Shortbread

THIS IS A DISH I REMEMBER MY GRAN MAKING. She also used to make Millionaire's Shortbread. I never told her which tasted the best, but I had to fight my sister for the burnt bits of this one on the oven tray.

MAKES 8

2 x 397g tins condensed milk
250g (9oz) unsalted butter,
  at room temperature
140g (5oz) caster sugar
140g (5oz) cornflour
300g (10¹/₂oz) plain flour
4 large bananas, peeled and
  chopped

FOR THE CARAMEL SAUCE
85g (3oz) caster sugar
100ml (3¹/₂fl oz) water

TO SERVE
vanilla ice-cream
fresh mint

1 Put the tins of condensed milk in a deep saucepan and cover with water. Bring to the boil, then reduce the heat and put on the lid. Leave to simmer rapidly for 2 hours, topping up the water if necessary – it's important it doesn't boil dry. Cool down completely before you open the tins to find a golden sticky caramel. (Once cooked, a tin of caramelised condensed milk will keep in the fridge for two weeks.)

2 Preheat the oven to 200°C/400°F/Gas 6. Cream the butter with the sugar until light and fluffy. Sift together the flours, then combine with the butter and sugar to form a dough. Gently knead until it all comes together in a firm ball.

3 Line a 20 x 30cm (8 x 12in) baking tin with nonstick baking parchment. Roll out two-thirds of the dough to fit the tin and lay it inside, pressing it neatly into the edges. Spread three-quarters of the caramelised condensed milk evenly over the base. Add the banana, then crumble the remaining third of the dough over the top.

4 Bake for 20–25 minutes. The caramel should have bubbled up a little among the dough and the top of the shortbread should be golden. Leave it to cool in the tin for 5 minutes before cutting it into 7.5cm (3in) squares, then leave to cool completely in the tin.

5 To make the caramel sauce, place the sugar in a clean, dry pan. Heat gently until the sugar melts and turns a light caramel colour. Carefully pour in the water, stir, then bring to the boil. Allow to cool.

6 Remove the squares from the tin and reheat them gently in the oven before serving with vanilla ice-cream, a sprig of fresh mint and a drizzle of the caramel sauce.

Jam Shortbreads

THESE ARE DELICATE AND, ONCE MADE, NEED TO BE HANDLED WITH CARE, as otherwise they will drop to bits. To do this, let them cool right down in the tins before turning them out.

MAKES 20–24

90g (3¹/₄oz) icing sugar, plus extra
    for dusting
185g (6¹/₂oz) plain flour
60g (2¹/₄oz) cornflour
30g (1¹/₄oz) ground almonds
250g (9oz) unsalted butter, diced
few drops of almond essence
raspberry or strawberry jam

1 Preheat the oven to 180°C/350°F/Gas 4. Sift the icing sugar, flour and cornflour together into a bowl. Add the ground almonds, then using your fingers or food processor, rub or mix the butter in until there are no visible lumps. Pour in the almond essence and mix well.

2 Turn the mixture out on to a lightly floured surface and knead a few times, just to form a smooth dough.

3 Butter a muffin pan. Roll the dough into small balls and place them in the muffin cups, flattening the tops slightly with your fingers. The dough should come about one-third of the way up the side of the pan to give a nice proportion to the finished biscuit.

4 Bake the shortbreads until they are a light gold colour, about 8–12 minutes. Remove them from the oven and, with your thumb or a teaspoon, make a small indentation in the top of each biscuit. Let the shortbreads cool for a few minutes, then turn the mould over and tap it over the bench so that the shortbreads fall out. Be gentle, as they are fragile while they are still warm. Leave to cool.

5 Dust the tops of the shortbreads with extra icing sugar using a shaker or sieve. Then, using a teaspoon, fill the indentation with jam or your chosen filling.

Parkin

IN YORKSHIRE WE USED TO EAT THIS ON BONFIRE NIGHT, and it is one of those cakes, like ginger cake, that gets better after three to four days in a tin. It's dark and rich and, once cut into squares and placed in a sealed tin, becomes moister and eats even better.

SERVES 4

225g (8oz) self-raising flour
115g (4oz) caster sugar
2 tsp ground ginger
1 tsp bicarbonate of soda
55g (2oz) butter
115g (4oz) golden syrup
1 free-range egg
200ml (7fl oz) milk

1 Preheat the oven to 150°C/300°F/Gas 2. Line a 20cm (8in) cake tin with greaseproof paper.

2 Sieve the flour, sugar, ginger and bicarbonate of soda into a bowl.

3 In a small pan, gently heat the butter and syrup until melted. Beat the egg into the milk.

4 Gradually pour the butter and syrup into the flour mixture and stir well. Pour in the egg and milk mixture and combine until smooth.

5 Pour into the lined tin and bake for 1 hour.

Brandy Snaps with Whipped Cream

I USED TO EAT LOADS OF THESE AS A KID. WORST OF ALL, my mother would bring a plate through while all my mates were round watching the telly and playing Atari and track-and-field on the Commodore 64 (that's an old computer to anyone who hasn't lived!). I used to sit and watch them devour the snaps one by one, thinking how much my fingers hurt from trying to make Daley Thompson do the 110-metre hurdles, and how they could eat them without a care in the world, because when I went to their houses you were lucky if you got a pear drop.

MAKES 30

225g (8oz) caster sugar
2 pinches of ground ginger
125g (4¹/₂oz) unsalted butter,
*   softened*
115g (4oz) plain flour
115g (4oz) golden syrup

TO SERVE
600ml (1 pint) double cream,
*   whipped*

1 Slightly cream together the sugar, ginger and butter. Add the flour and golden syrup, and mix to a firm paste. Roll into a long sausage about 4cm (1½in) in diameter, then wrap tightly in clingfilm, making sure not to catch the clingfilm inside the roll. Chill well (overnight is best).

2 Preheat the oven to 180°C/350°F/Gas 4. Lightly grease a baking tray.

3 Remove the clingfilm from the sausage and cut off 5mm (¼in) thick slices. Arrange the slices on the baking tray, spacing them out well. Bake for about 8–10 minutes, or until well spread out and golden.

4 Remove from the oven and leave to cool for a few seconds to firm up slightly. Using a spatula or fish slice, carefully remove one brandy snap at a time from the baking sheet, then straight away loosely wrap it around the handle of a wooden spoon to shape into a roll. (If the brandy snaps cool too quickly and start to break, a good tip is to put them back in the oven for a minute or so to soften slightly.) Slide the brandy snaps off the spoon handles and leave to cool. Store in an airtight container for 3 or 4 days.

5 To serve, fill with plain old whipped double cream.

Carrot Cake

CARROT CAKE IS GOOD EATEN WITH SLIGHTLY WHIPPED CREAM. In the States they make a heavier, darker version than this. The cake is at its best served simply.

MAKES 1 CAKE

butter, for greasing
5 medium carrots, trimmed,
  scraped and sliced
juice of 2 oranges
125ml (4fl oz) corn oil
4 free-range eggs, separated
375g (13oz) caster sugar
350g (12oz) '00' pasta flour,
  or plain flour
15g (¹/₂oz) baking powder

TO SERVE
200ml (7fl oz) double cream
2–3 tsp Cointreau

1 Preheat the oven to 180°C/350°F/Gas 4 and butter a cake tin of 30cm (12in) in diameter.

2 Put the carrot in a pan, cover with water and add the orange juice. Bring to the boil and cook until tender. Drain and cool, then discard the liquid. Put the carrots in a blender with the corn oil and the four egg yolks, and whizz to a purée. Transfer to a bowl.

3 Beat the egg whites until stiff, and set aside.

4 In another bowl, mix the sugar, flour and baking powder together, then fold into the carrot purée, until well combined. Now gently fold in the egg whites. Pour the mixture into the prepared tin and bake for 30-35 minutes.

5 When the cake is cooked, take it out of the oven and leave to cool on a wire rack.

6 Whip the double cream and stir in the Cointreau. Cut a slice of cake and serve with a dollop of the cream.

Madeira Cake

I REMEMBER MY AUNTIE MAKING THIS CAKE AT CHRISTMAS. She used to eat it with a glass of Madeira, and dunk it in the glass. Then she'd down the remains, crumbs and all, with a smile on her face – whether because of the wine or the cake, I don't know, but possibly as a result of both…

MAKES 1 X 18CM CAKE

175g (6oz) butter, plus
* extra for greasing*
175g (6oz) caster sugar
3 large free-range eggs
250g (9oz) self-raising flour
about 3 tbsp milk
finely grated zest of 1 lemon
several thin pieces of candied
* citron or lemon peel, to decorate*

1 Preheat the oven to 180°C/350°F/Gas 4. Grease a 900g (2lb) bread or cake tin, line the base and sides with greaseproof paper and grease the paper.

2 Cream the butter and sugar together in a bowl until pale and fluffy. Beat in the eggs, one at a time, beating the mixture well between each one and adding a tablespoon of the flour with the last egg to prevent the mixture curdling.

3 Sift the flour and gently fold in with enough milk to give a mixture that falls reluctantly from the spoon. Fold in the lemon zest. Spoon the mixture into the prepared tin and lightly level the top. Bake on the middle shelf of the oven for 30 minutes.

4 Place the candied peel on top of the cake and bake for a further 30 minutes, or until a warm skewer inserted into the centre comes out clean. Leave the cake to cool in the tin for 10 minutes, then turn it out on to a wire rack and leave to cool completely.

JAMS, CHUTNEYS, AND SAUCES

Cross Butts Farm shop in Whitby

CALL AGAIN
OPENING TIMES
7 DAYS A WEEK
9 - 5.30
FRESH FARM
PRODUCE
EGGS
50p
P.R.B. MEGGINSON 1972

Raspberry Jam

MAKING JAM IS A BRILLIANT WAY OF USING UP FRESH SEASONAL FRUIT. This is one of my favourites.

MAKES 1.2KG (2¾LB)

600g (1lb 5oz) jam sugar
juice and finely grated zest of
*   1 lemon*
1kg (2¼lb) fresh raspberries,
*   picked over carefully*

1 To sterilise the jam jars, place them in a large pan and cover them with cold water. Bring to the boil and simmer for 10–15 minutes. Remove from the water and leave upside down to dry.

2 Place the sugar and the lemon juice and zest in a large pan and heat very slowly until the sugar has melted.

3 Add the raspberries and stir gently. Bring to the boil and cook for 3–4 minutes, or 10 minutes if you prefer a thicker style of jam.

4 Leave to cool slightly, skimming off any froth with a clean spoon. Spoon into the sterilised jars, seal immediately and label when cool.

Sweet and Sour Grape Pickle

HOME-MADE PICKLES BEAT STORE-CUPBOARD ONES ANY DAY. There is nothing better than reaching for a jar of your own pickles to add that extra kick to your meal!

MAKES 1 LITRE
(1¾ PINTS)

750g (1lb 10oz) seedless white grapes
10 sprigs of fresh tarragon
500ml (18fl oz) champagne vinegar or white wine vinegar
175ml (6fl oz) honey
1 tsp salt

1 Wash the grapes well and then dry them. Put them in a large sterilised preserving jar with the sprigs of tarragon (*see opposite* for sterilising instructions).

2 Boil the vinegar and honey together for 2 minutes, then add the salt and pour the mixture over the grapes. Seal the jar immediately and label when cool.

3 For the best results, store in a cool dark place for up to 1 month before opening.

Plum Chutney

GIVE ME CHUTNEYS, CHUTNEYS AND MORE CHUTNEYS … I make this one from the plums from my trees in the garden. They are the dark flesh and skin type. If you can't get those, any plums will do, as this is a simple and quick way of making chutney.

MAKES 350G (12OZ)

500g (18oz) dark red plums
2 shallots, peeled and chopped
1 tbsp olive oil
100ml (3¹/₂fl oz) white wine vinegar
3 tbsp water
1 cinnamon stick
100g (3¹/₂oz) demerara sugar

1 Cut the plums in half down the crease, twist the halves in opposite directions and pull apart. Prise out the stones and discard. Roughly chop the flesh.

2 Place the shallots in a heavy-based saucepan with the oil and heat until sizzling. Sauté gently for 5 minutes until softened.

3 Add the plums, vinegar, water, cinnamon stick and sugar. Stir until the sugar is dissolved, then simmer for about 15 minutes, stirring occasionally, until softened and slightly thickened.

4 Meanwhile, heat the oven to 110–120ºC/225–250ºF/Gas ¼–½. Place a sterilised jam jar in the oven to warm (*see page* 130 for sterilising instructions). When the plum chutney is ready, spoon it into the jar. Seal with a lid and leave to cool completely before labelling.

Pear Chutney

I DID SAY I liked chutney!

MAKES 900G (2LB)

4 tbsp olive oil
1 tsp finely chopped fresh
*   rosemary*
200g (7oz) sultanas
100g (3¹/₂oz) raisins
100g (3¹/₂oz) demerara sugar
400ml (14fl oz) cider vinegar
100g (3¹/₂oz) crystallised ginger,
*   finely sliced*
800g (1³/₄lb) pears, cored
*   and cut into wedges*
¹/₂ tsp salt
¹/₂ tsp freshly grated nutmeg
2 tsp ground allspice
good pinch of saffron strands

1 Heat a preserving pan and add the oil, rosemary, sultanas, raisins and sugar. Fry them until the fruit begins to caramelise.

2 Pour in the vinegar and boil on a high heat for 3 minutes. Add the rest of the ingredients, bring to the boil, then turn down to a simmer and cook until most of the liquid has evaporated. Because of the fruit, this chutney has a tendency to stick to the bottom of the pan, so stir it well and keep an eye on it.

3 Spoon into hot, sterilised jars, filling them as full as you can, and seal while hot (*see page* 130 for sterilising instructions). Label and store in the fridge when cool. It is important not to cook this too much as the pear wedges need to keep their nice shape.

Gooseberry, Raisin and Green Peppercorn Chutney

YET ANOTHER ONE, particularly good with grilled fish such as mackerel or tuna. It also goes with most cheeses.

MAKES 900G (2LB)

600g (1lb 5oz) fresh gooseberries
2 medium onions, peeled
   and chopped
1 garlic clove, peeled and crushed
1/2 tsp mustard powder
juice of 1/2 lemon
300ml (10fl oz) cider vinegar
   or white wine vinegar
200g (7oz) raisins
large pinch of salt
275g (91/2oz) soft brown sugar
3 tbsp green peppercorns

1 Put the gooseberries, onions, garlic, mustard and lemon juice in a preserving pan and pour in two-thirds of the vinegar. Bring to the boil, then reduce the heat and simmer for about 45 minutes, stirring occasionally, until thick.

2 Add the raisins, salt, sugar and the rest of the vinegar. Stir over a low heat until the sugar has dissolved, then simmer for up to 1 hour, stirring frequently, until thick and syrupy.

3 Stir in the peppercorns, then remove from the heat. Pour immediately into hot, sterilised jars, and seal (*see page* 130 for sterilising instructions). Label and store in a cool, dark place.

Courgette and Black Peppercorn Chutney

I LOVE THIS RECIPE, which I came across while in Yorkshire filming in this man's garden allotment. He was an amazing gardener who taught me the ins and outs of the carrot and the humble spud. His wife was an equally amazing cook, and she gave me a jar of this courgette chutney. I took it home, but didn't try it until some 4 months later. It was so good I tracked them down again, and she kindly gave me her recipe.

MAKES 900G (2LB)

2 small lemons
3 medium courgettes
2 onions, peeled and thinly sliced
100ml (3½fl oz) dry white wine
3 tsp brown sugar
24 black peppercorns,
 coarsely crushed
2.5cm (1in) piece of fresh root
 ginger, peeled and finely
 chopped
good pinch of salt

1 Peel the lemons, cutting away all the pith, then slice them thinly and discard the pips. Cut the courgettes in half lengthways, then across into 2.5cm (1in) pieces.

2 Combine all the ingredients in a preserving pan. Cover and cook over a moderate heat for 1 hour, stirring from time to time. There will be quite a bit of liquid at the end of the cooking time, but once the chutney has cooled, the consistency will be perfect.

3 Either bottle in hot, sterilised jars, or put in a bowl to serve (*see page 130 for sterilising instructions*).

Tomato and Apple Chutney

I LOVE THIS WITH JUST CHEESE ON ITS OWN or even with some pan-fried cod or salmon.

MAKES 1.8KG (4LB)

300ml (10fl oz) malt vinegar
225g (8oz) brown sugar
100g (3½oz) sultanas
2.5cm (1in) piece of fresh root
   ginger, peeled and finely
   chopped
2 red chillies, seeded and chopped
1kg (2¼lb) red tomatoes, roughly
   chopped
250g (9oz) apples, peeled, cored
   and chopped
200g (7oz) chunky shallots, peeled
   and roughly chopped
salt and freshly ground
   black pepper

1 Place the vinegar and sugar in a preserving pan and heat on the stove to reduce a little. Add the sultanas and cook until the vinegar and sugar start to caramelise. Add all the other ingredients, and bring to a simmer. Cover and cook gently for 20–30 minutes, stirring all the time.

2 Leave the chutney chunky, and not overcooked, which would make it more like a purée. Spoon into hot, sterilised jars, and label when cool (*see page* 130 for sterilising instructions).

Hollandaise Sauce

THIS IS ONE OF THE FIRST SAUCES YOU LEARN TO MAKE AS A CHEF. It should never be overheated, otherwise the butter will split. Asparagus is great with this, as are poached eggs.

Clarified butter is what you get when it separates from the whey. To do this, place the butter in a small pan and leave it over a very low heat until it has melted. Skim off any scum from the surface, and pour off the clear (clarified) butter into a bowl, leaving behind the milky white solids that will have settled on the bottom. These should be discarded.

SERVES 4

2 tbsp water
2 free-range egg yolks
225g (8oz) clarified butter, warmed
juice of 1/2 lemon
good pinch of cayenne pepper
1/2 tsp salt

1 Put the water and egg yolks into a stainless-steel or glass bowl set over a pan of simmering water, making sure that the base of the bowl is not touching the water. Whisk until voluminous and creamy.

2 Remove the bowl from the pan and gradually whisk in the clarified butter until thick. Then whisk in the lemon juice, cayenne pepper and salt.

3 This sauce is best used as soon as it is made, but will hold for up to 2 hours if kept covered in a warm place, such as over a pan of water.

QUICK HOLLANDAISE SAUCE

Using the same quantities as above, put the water, egg yolks and lemon juice and into a liquidiser. Turn on the machine, then slowly pour the warm butter through the lid. Season with cayenne pepper and salt.

Barbecue Sauce

IF PEOPLE KNEW BARBECUE SAUCE WAS THIS EASY TO MAKE, they wouldn't be buying ready-made stuff in bottles. If you're using this for barbecued food, don't use it all for the marinade. It is best to baste this on while the food is cooking and serve with some of the same sauce on the side.

ACCOMPANIES 1.8KG (4LB) PORK SPARE RIBS

1 onion, peeled and chopped
3 garlic cloves, peeled and crushed
2 tbsp olive oil
1 fresh red chilli, seeded and
    finely chopped
1 tsp fennel seeds, crushed
55g (2oz) dark brown sugar
50ml (2fl oz) dark soy sauce
300ml (10fl oz) tomato ketchup
salt and freshly ground
    black pepper

1 Fry the onion and garlic in the olive oil with the chilli, fennel seeds and sugar.

2 Add the soy sauce and ketchup, and season with salt and pepper. Bring to the boil and simmer for a few minutes to amalgamate the flavours.

Home-made Tomato Ketchup

TRY THIS WITH KIDS WHEN THEY'RE YOUNG and they will know what real home-made food tastes like.

MAKES 600ML (1 PINT)

250ml (9fl oz) cider or white
    wine vinegar
7 tbsp demerara or caster sugar
1 clove
1/4 tsp ground coriander
1/4 tsp ground cinnamon
1 bay leaf
1.5kg (3lb 5oz) ripe tomatoes,
    net weight after quartering and
    seeding
2 tsp salt
1 tbsp mustard powder
1 garlic clove, peeled and crushed
dash of Tabasco sauce
2 tbsp tomato purée
freshly ground black pepper

1 Place the vinegar and sugar in a heavy-based pan and bring to a simmer with the spices and bay leaf. Add the rest of the ingredients and bring to the boil, stirring to prevent any sticking. Once up to the boil, reduce the temperature and simmer, stirring occasionally, for 40 minutes. Be careful the mix doesn't stick to the base of the pan.

2 Blitz in a food processor or liquidiser. Push the sauce through a sieve.

3 If you find the sauce to be loose and thin once cold, simply reboil and thicken with a little cornflour or arrowroot mixed to a paste with water. Don't make it too thick though, as this last step is just to prevent the tomato water separating from the sauce.

Home-made Salad Cream

I KNOW WHAT YOU'RE ALL THINKING. Why should I make my own when I can buy it in a bottle? But like the tomato ketchup, don't make that decision until you have tried making it. If refrigerated, this sauce will keep for a minimum of 1–2 weeks.

MAKES 200–300ML (7–10FL OZ)

1 tbsp plain flour
4 tsp caster sugar
2 tsp mustard powder
a pinch of salt
2 free-range eggs
100ml (3¹/₂fl oz) white wine vinegar
150ml (5fl oz) double cream
squeeze of lemon juice

1 Mix together the flour, sugar, mustard and salt in a bowl. Beat in the eggs and white wine vinegar.

2 Place the bowl over a pan of simmering water and stir until warmed and thickened. This will take only 4–5 minutes. Once 'cooked', remove the bowl from the heat and leave to cool.

3 Now it is time to add the cream. With this you can be as generous as you wish. A minimum of 100ml (3¹/₂fl oz) will be needed. Finish with a squeeze of lemon juice and the salad cream is ready.

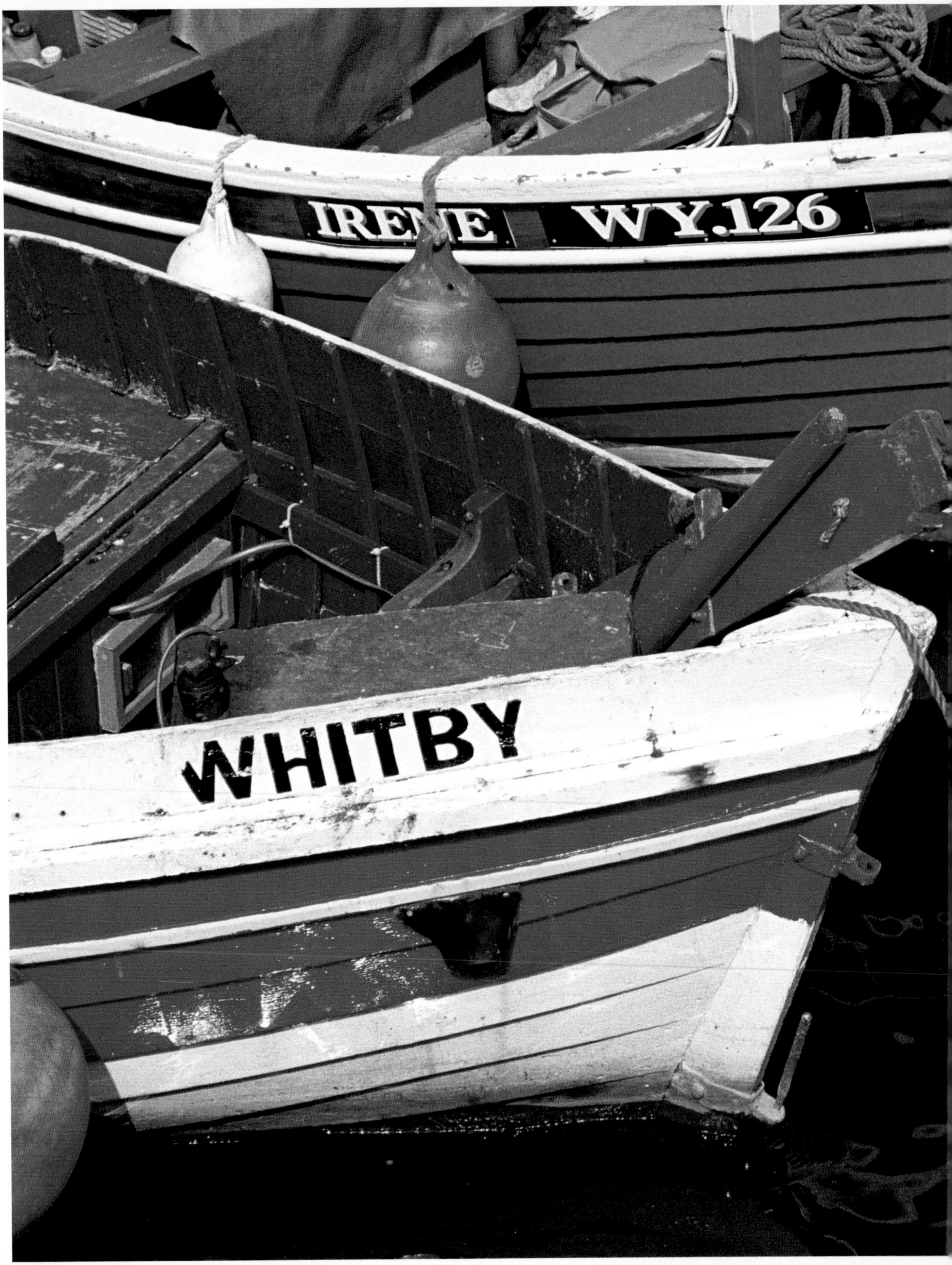
IRENE
WY.126
WHITBY